10 Best Teaching Practices

Second Edition

To my sons, Christopher Scott McBrayer and Kevin Lane McBrayer,
and in memory of their brother, Chad Michael McBrayer.

10 Best Teaching Practices

How Brain Research,
Learning Styles,
and Standards
Define Teaching
Competencies

Second Edition

DONNA WALKER TILESTON

CORWIN PRESS
A SAGE Publications Company
Thousand Oaks, California

For information:

Corwin Press
A Sage Publications Company
2455 Teller Road
Thousand Oaks, California 91320
E-mail: order@corwinpress.com

Sage Publications Ltd.
1 Oliver's Yard
55 City Road
London, EC1Y 1SP
United Kingdom

Sage Publications India Pvt. Ltd.
B-42, Panchsheel Enclave
Post Box 4109
New Delhi 110 017 India

Printed in the United States of America

Library of Congress Cataloging-in-Publication Data

Tileston, Donna Walker.
Ten best teaching practices: how brain research, learning styles, and standards define teaching competencies / Donna Walker Tileston.— 2nd ed.
    p. cm.
Rev. ed. of: 10 best teaching practices. c2000.
Includes bibliographical references and index.
ISBN 1-4129-1471-X (cloth) — ISBN 1-4129-1472-8 (pbk.)
  1. Effective teaching—United States. 2. Learning. 3. Educational innovations—United States. 4. Educational change—United States. I. Tileston, Donna Walker. 10 best teaching practices. II. Title.
LB1775.2.T54 2005
371.102—dc22

                          2004026178

This book is printed on acid-free paper.

05   06   07   08   09   10   9   8   7   6   5   4   3   2   1

Acquisitions Editor:	Faye Zucker
Editorial Assistant:	Gem Rabanera
Production Editor:	Tracy Alpern
Copy Editor:	Stacey Shimizu
Proofreader:	Nevair Kabakian
Typesetter:	C&M Digitals (P) Ltd.
Indexer:	Kay Dusheck
Cover Designer:	Michael Dubowe
Graphic Designer:	Lisa Miller

Contents

Preface

The ultimate source of exceptional performance is exceptional learning. Therefore, the question is how can we best produce exceptional learning in young people? How can we make exceptional learning unexceptional?

—Laurence Hooper, *The Wall Street Journal* (1992)

We live in a time in which a revolution in education is occurring. Through brain research and technology, we have unlocked many of the reasons why some children experience so much difficulty in learning. We know more about effective teaching practices than at any other time in history. Through technological advances, we have a whole world as our resource base. In addition, teachers are finally being empowered to make the choices that affect their classrooms.

Although we have tremendous resources available to us, schools have been slow to use that information to change the way classes are conducted. We live in an age in which vast amounts of information must be assimilated, synthesized, and communicated, yet too many schools continue to teach with the methods of the 1950s . . . rote memorization of dates, places, and facts that are quickly forgotten after "the test." It is no wonder that we are losing our students and that they enter a world ill prepared for the information explosion. As we shift to a new age and a vastly different approach in the way businesses operate, we must also shift our thinking. The Association for Supervision and Curriculum Development (ASCD, 1999a) says, "In 10 years, there will be two kinds of people: the well educated and the hardly employable." Knowledge and technology will be the great equalizers of this millennium. Education has a responsibility to see that students have, at a minimum, the knowledge base they need to be "players" on a level playing field.

This book is written to incorporate the brain research, the learning styles information, and the issue of standards into a classroom instructional model. It is not intended to be a technical manual on the brain; the bookstores are filled with books that do a good job of giving us the technical research. Rather, this book is a look at the application of the brain research and how it can be applied to the classroom. We have wonderful research available to us, but reading and discussing it is not enough: We must get it to the people who can benefit the most—our students. We will reach our students only when we incorporate the knowledge base we have into classroom practices.

I have identified 10 teaching practices that have tremendous power in the classroom when we incorporate the best of research with their implementation. These teaching strategies are based on the best research in the field and on real classroom experience by practitioners. More than 15 years ago, I began a dynamic field study on the factors that enhance learning and the factors that impede it. Along with a group of teachers, I used the research that was available at that time to help restructure a school in trouble. Positive results could be seen almost immediately and have been sustained over the years. Today, the school that once had low test scores, a high dropout rate, and many discipline problems enjoys some of the highest test scores in the state, SAT and ACT scores well above the state and national average, and low incidences of discipline problems. What is significant about this study is that the results have been sustained over time—it was not a one-shot quick fix, but a systemic process that has grown. The new research on how the brain learns has validated the structures that we put in place and built over the past two decades.

I am writing this book for educators, to tell you that success is possible in your school. In the chapters that follow, I will examine 10 practices that are essential if we are to make education meaningful and rich. It is a process that takes time, training, resources, and commitment, but it is worth it because it raises the quality of life for kids.

Chapter 1 looks at the importance of a climate that is enriched and emotionally supportive. The brain research on the effects of climate and the brain's capacity to learn is critical. Not only can we reverse the effects of an early negative environment, but, according to Sousa (1995), we can actually increase the IQ scores of students by as much as 20 points by enhancing the environment for learning. I consider this chapter to be critical, because if we cannot create a climate in which all students feel physically and emotionally secure, the rest doesn't matter.

Chapter 2 addresses the need for a wide repertoire of teaching techniques so that all students, regardless of learning modality, will be successful. Schools of the past taught mainly to the auditory learners; schools of the future must teach to all learners. New research shows that as much as 80% of the classroom may be made up of students who don't learn auditorily (Sousa, 2001). We must examine not only the three modalities for incoming information, but the rhythm of the teaching as well. The attention span of the brain follows a rhythm that, if incorporated into the time frame of teaching, ensures greater response from students.

Chapter 3 looks at the critical element of connections or transfers in learning. The brain is a seeker of connections, and where they do not exist, there is chaos. Our job as educators is to build on connections that already exist and to help create connections where there are none. This chapter offers hope to the parents, teachers, and students as they search for ways to put learning into long-term memory.

Chapter 4 is an investigation into the workings of the memory system. How does the brain decide what to toss and what to keep? More important, how can we take this new knowledge to the classroom? All of us, as educators, have experienced those agonizing moments when we realized that although we taught our hearts out, the students just didn't get it. With the mystery of how we learn and remember solved, teachers of the future have the opportunity to make learning more meaningful than at any other time in history.

Chapter 5 looks at the need to provide motivating, challenging work in the classroom. The days of meaningless busywork must be brought to a close. Time is too precious a commodity to waste in the classroom. Our students will enter a world in which computers can do rote memory tasks. We must prepare them for the things computers cannot do—problem solving, complex thinking, and collaboration.

Chapter 6 is a discussion of the power of true collaborative learning. In the global world, the need for articulation skills, the ability to work with a variety of people, and the ability to collaborate on problem solving is critical. What a wonderful gift to give to our students! Studies from Marian Diamond (1998) show that we thrive when we learn in social settings.

Chapter 7 discusses the importance of success for all learners. We must take a hard look at student data in its desegregated form. We must look at cultural differences and the research on what works and what does not. It's time to bring in the experts and it is time to be honest about what is not working.

Chapter 8 identifies what authentic assessment is and what it is not. We must move away from assessment that is short term and influenced by rote memory alone to a process that is ongoing and that truly tests long-term memory. We must begin to assess learning in the context of how it is going to be used. Only then can we truly know if students can use the information.

Chapter 9 looks at relevance as it applies to learning. Like climate, this is one of the most powerful areas of influence on how and whether the brain learns and remembers. It is the answer for those who ask, "When are we ever going to use this?"

Chapter 10 is a look into the future to an anytime, anywhere learning space. Technology is an integral part of the home and workplace. Schools must get on board and learn to use productivity tools to lead students to more complex work.

In Chapter 11, I provide some closing remarks based on the findings in this book and on the research from the school that we restructured more than 15 years ago. A true test for any restructured school is whether students are successful and, if so, whether they are successful over time. Students in our school began to show remarkable improvement almost immediately and have built on that success over time. When we began years ago to restructure this school, we did it based on the knowledge available at that time. We did not know many of the things that we now know about how the brain works; we applied what we knew worked for kids and then built on it as new information became available. Our instincts were correct. As these principles apply in that school, I believe they can apply in any school in the country.

About the Author

 **Donna Walker Tileston** is a veteran teacher of three decades, a best-selling and award-winning author, and a full-time consultant. She is the President of Strategic Teaching & Learning, which provides services to schools throughout the United States and Canada. She is the author of *Strategies for Teaching Differently: On the Block or Not* (Corwin Press, 1998), *Innovative Strategies of the Block Schedule* (Bureau of Education and Research [BER], 1999), *What Every Teacher Should Know: The 10-Book Collection* (Corwin Press, 2004), which won the Association of Educational Publishers' 2004 Distinguished Achievement Award as a Professional Development Handbook.

She received her bachelor's degree from The University of North Texas, her master's from East Texas State University, and her doctorate from Texas A&M University, Commerce. She may be reached at www.strategicteachinglearning.com or by e-mail at dwtileston@yahoo.com.

Creating an Environment That Facilitates Learning

An enriched and supportive environment is so important that none of the other techniques discussed will be really effective unless the issues of enrichment and support are addressed first. In a world full of broken relationships, broken promises, and broken hearts, a strong supportive relationship is important to students. While we cannot control the students' environments outside the classroom, we have tremendous control over their environment for 7 hours each day. We have the power to create positive or negative images about education, to develop an enriched environment, and to become the catalysts for active learning. We now know that how we feel about education has great impact on how the brain reacts to it. Emotion and cognitive learning are not separate entities; they work in tandem with one another.

—Donna Walker Tileston, *Ten Best Teaching Practices* (2000)

S tudents enter our classrooms with a great deal going on in the brain that has nothing to do with the learning at hand. They may have had an argument at home before school or a negative experience in the hallway. They may be excited about an upcoming event or a new boyfriend or girlfriend. As teachers, we have a great deal of competition for our students' attention. Most of us were taught to begin our teaching with the cognitive center of the brain. It is no wonder that teachers all over the country lament the fact that students are not motivated to learn. The motivation to learn is controlled by the self-system of the brain, not the cognitive system. Let me say that again: All learning

Figure 1.1 The Systems of Thinking

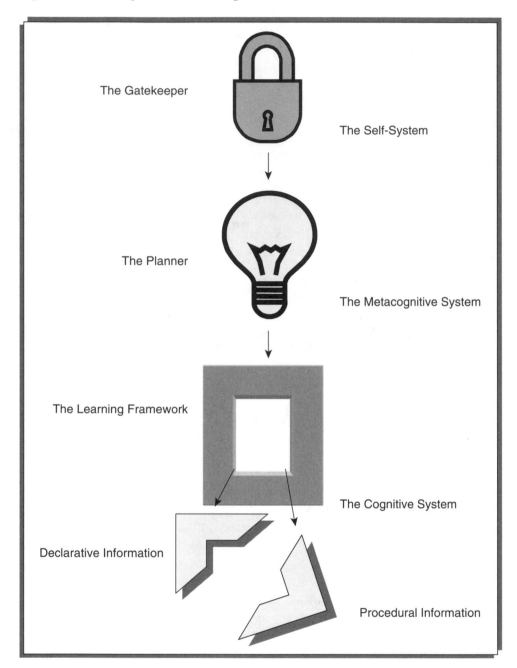

begins in the self-system of the brain. It is this system that decides whether the student will pay attention and whether the student will begin a task. Once the decision has been made to pay attention or begin a task, the metacognitive system of the brain takes over and makes a plan for carrying out the work. Only then is the cognitive system employed. Figure 1.1 is a graphic representation of this process.

As teachers, we need to be cognizant of the fact that the decision whether or not to engage in the learning is going to take place with or without us. We can influence that decision by the way we approach the teaching and learning process. According to Tileston (2004a), the following three criteria are critical to the decision by the brain to pay attention to the learning.

THE PERSONAL IMPORTANCE OF THE LEARNING TO THE STUDENT

No one will argue that learning is important. However, for learning to be addressed by the brain, it must be perceived as important to the individual. The first criterion is that the student must believe the learning satisfies a personal need or goal. Marzano (2001a) explains it this way: "What an individual considers to be important is probably a function of the extent to which it meets one of two conditions: it is perceived as instrumental in satisfying a basic need, or it is perceived as instrumental in the attainment of a personal goal."

How many of us have heard students say, "When are we ever going to use this?" Students today are in overload on information; if they only need to know it for the test on Friday, then they will memorize it long enough to put it on the test and then promptly forget it. If it has real-world meaning to them, it is more likely to be placed into long-term memory. Begin units of study by helping students see the importance of the learning to them personally. Personal importance may be viewed in many ways. Some examples include the following:

- *Personal goals that address immediate needs.* For example, if students from the inner city learn basic math facts, this will help prevent them from being cheated on the street. Another example would be a student who is about to take an exam for advanced credit. This student is more apt to pay attention to learning that will help him or her prepare for the test.

- *Personal goals that increase the esteem of the student to a particular group.* For example, a student who wants to impress friends or gain the attention or affection of parents or of a school group will pay more attention to those topics that are of importance to the other individuals or groups.

- *Personal goals that are long term in nature.* For example, students may not see the relevance of studying slope in their immediate lives, but may realize that they must know this information to get into a higher-math class later on. Another student may want to work in international finance and thus sees the importance of learning about the cultures of other countries.

THE DEVELOPMENT OF SELF-EFFICACY IN THE LEARNER

The second criterion that is examined by the brain is called *self-efficacy*. Self-efficacy differs from self-esteem in that self-esteem is based on a feeling or belief about oneself that may or may not have been proven. I may believe that I can do the work even though I have never tried it before. While this is important, self-efficacy is more powerful because it is based on fact: I know that I can do the more difficult math assignment because I have had success with math before. This is one of the reasons why it is so important for students to experience success—even incremental success—in the classroom. Success really does breed success.

Self-efficacy is also the belief that one has the capacity to be successful. Capacity is based on ability, resources, and power over the situation. A student may believe that he or she can do the math assignment, but may not have enough directions (resources) to carry it out. Many students will give up at this point. Another example would be a student who believes that he or she has the ability and the resources but cannot complete the assignment because the home environment does not allows them to work. While we cannot change the home environment, we can help provide a place to work. Some of the ways that the classroom teacher can build self-efficacy include the following:

- *Provide opportunities for success.* This does not mean "watering down the information." Giving students an inferior education does not build self-esteem or self-efficacy. Give students the capacity to be successful and then provide feedback often. Feedback should include both positive reinforcement (what they are doing correctly) and suggestions for improvement as needed. Just saying "good job" is not feedback.

- *Build capacity in students by providing adequate directions and opportunities to practice the learning.* Be sure that there is adequate time for the learning to take place and that students have been given feedback.

- *Encourage students to develop their own goals for the learning.* Do this by modeling. Place your goals for the learning in the classroom so that students can see the goals. Go back to the goals often so that students can see their progress. For nonreaders, use symbols for the learning and send the objectives for the units home to parents. Post learning goals on the Internet or Intranet at your learning site.

- *Provide students with the expectations for the learning up front, before the learning begins.* Do this in writing when possible. The expectations might be in the form of a matrix or rubric, or they might simply be written out and given to the learners. By doing this, teachers get rid of the "gotchas," in which students are assessed for something that they did not learn.

HOW STUDENTS FEEL ABOUT THE LEARNING, CLASSROOM, SUBJECT MATTER, AND THE OTHER STUDENTS

If you have ever been in a classroom in which the emotional climate was one of tension or fear, you already know why the third criterion, how students feel about the learning, is so important. Our species has survived because our brain attends to information by priority. If we are under threat, whether physical, emotional or otherwise, our brain pays attention to the threat over all other incoming stimuli. As Jensen (1997) says, "The brain stem is the part of the brain that directs your behavior under negative stress; and is the most responsive to any threat. When threat is perceived, excessive cortisol is released into the body causing higher-order thinking to take a backseat to automatic functions that may help you survive." Goleman (1995), in his book *Emotional Intelligence,* talks about the effects of stress over time. He says that when an individual is under stress he or she cannot remember, learn or make decisions clearly because "stress makes us stupid."

Not all of these criteria are equal in weight. For example, a student may not see the importance of learning about slope in mathematics but likes the class, respects the teacher, and has had positive experiences in math in the past, and so the student may choose to give the subject a chance to prove to him or her that it is relevant. Marzano (2001a) says, "If the task is judged important, if the probability of success is high, and if positive affect is generated or associated with the task, the individual will be motivated to engage in the new task. If the new task is evaluated as having low relevance and/or low probability of success and has an associated negative effect, motivation to engage in the task is low."

Figure 1.2 is a graphic model that depicts, in simple terms, the decision-making process going on in the brain during the self-system phase of the learning.

Although a goal in education is to promote learning, sometimes outside factors inhibit the process. One of these inhibitors is stress, and a common reason for stress in students is threat. Jensen (1998) says, "Threat impairs brain cells. Threat also changes the body's chemistry and impacts learning." Stress chemicals act on the hippocampus, the part of the brain that filters and helps store long-term factual memories. Some examples of threat in the classroom include anything that embarrasses a student, unrealistic deadlines, a student's inability to speak a language, inappropriate learning styles, and an uncomfortable classroom culture (Jensen, 1998).

Years ago, I was involved in a restructuring project in a high school that proved to me the enormous impact of positive climate on student learning. Our faculty had come to a point of desperation: We knew students were not learning at a quality level and we knew they did not want to come to school. Our high dropout rate was proof. We understood how the students felt, because we too were burned out. Our test scores were average at best; in addition to the high dropout rate, we had a fledgling attendance rate and discipline problems. So, we came together, made a list of all the things we thought were wrong with school and a list of the things that were keeping it from being the kind of learning place we wanted to be. We did our homework. We studied the research and we called in the experts. We were actively involved in more than 15 days of training on the factors that enhance learning and the factors that impede it. As we came to know more about how children learn, we changed our attitude about teaching and learning, and we reinvented our school into the kind of place we believed school should be.

When our students came back in the fall, it was to an entirely different kind of school. On the first day of school, we stood in front of our classes and gave

Figure 1.2 Depiction of Self-System of the Brain

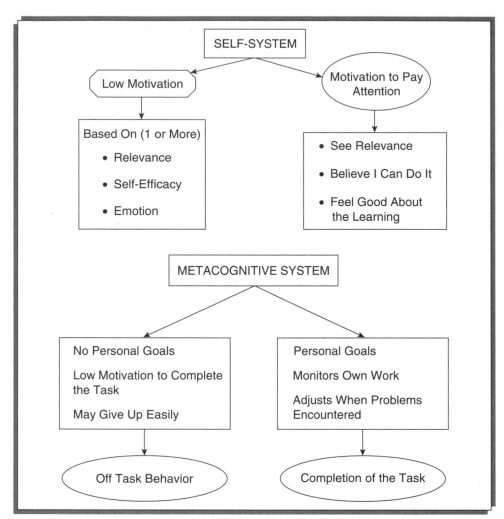

students a pep talk that would make any coach proud. We talked about how we believed in our students. We encouraged them to do their best work and we promised them that we would be the best teachers we had ever been. We told them that there would be no more "gotchas" in our school, that they would always be told what they needed to do to be successful in our classrooms—and if they did it, they would be successful. We quit teaching as if we were the all-knowing scribes and made the students active participants in the learning. We created real-world applications to the learning and we told students up front what the learning had to do with their world. We encouraged creativity, connections to the learning, and reflective thinking. We created a place where learning was respected and nourished—and we all thrived.

In October of that year, we gave our state exam, which students must pass in order to graduate. As a faculty, we told ourselves not to be discouraged if the scores were not improved over the prior year. After all, we had been teaching differently for only two months and there was no way we could make up for the lack of knowledge in such a short time. When the scores came back, there was so much improvement that we thought it was a fluke. In the past, only 28% of our at-risk students had mastered every part of the test on the first try. When our tests came back, 67% of our at-risk students mastered every part of the state test. We were baffled. We knew we could not have taught these students that much material in only two months!

In the winter, while in Austin, I attended a seminar on brain research conducted by Madeline Hunter. She talked first about the research of the 1970s into something called the *placebo effect*, in which a group of people were told that they were being given penicillin for a virus when, in fact, they were being given a placebo. Regardless, one third of them got well. Her new research showed that if the doctor giving the placebo believes that he is giving the group penicillin, and if he convinces the group of this, more than half of them will get well. I knew, then, what had happened to our at-risk students. For the first time, as a group, we believed that all kids could learn; we convinced the students of that fact, and more than half of them—67%—"got well." What a powerful influence emotion is on the brain. When we begin to tap into that power in schools, remarkable things are possible.

In his book *How the Brain Learns*, David Sousa (1995, 2001) talks about the importance of emotion on the brain. He says that emotional responses can actually diminish the brain's ability to process cognitive information:

> We have all had experiences when anger, fear of the unknown, or joy quickly overcame our rational thoughts. This override of conscious thought can be strong enough to cause temporary inability to talk . . . or move. This happens because the hippocampus is susceptible to stress hormones which can inhibit cognitive functioning and long-term memory.

Students who feel threatened in the classroom, whether physically or emotionally, are operating in a survival mode, and while learning can take place in that mode, it is with much difficulty. If a student feels that no matter what he does he can never please the teacher, if a student feels that no matter how hard she tries she can never understand the subject—whether the threat is real or perceived, that student will not ever be able to reach his or her potential in that environment.

Building a Brain-Friendly Environment

While we cannot control the lives of our students outside the classroom, as teachers, we can provide a quality environment for them each day. We do this by ensuring that the environment within our classrooms is enriched (meaningful, active engagement) and supportive. Factors that help create an enriched and supportive environment include the following: a sense of belonging, a high level of support for achievement, a sense of empowerment, more on-ramps, an advocate for every student, and resiliency in students.

A Sense of Belonging

All of us want to belong somewhere. We want to feel we are a part of the experience and that we are accepted. When students do not feel accepted, for whatever reason, they are more likely to find negative places to belong. That is what helps keep gangs active in our students' lives. Gangs and other negative influences fill a need that so often is not met in positive settings. As educators, we must create an environment in which students feel safe and accepted, an environment in which we are all learners together and where we feel a sense of togetherness—one where there are no "gotchas." Students are told up front what they must do to be successful, and then we must be faithful and hold them only to the criteria that we set.

Give students the tools they need to be successful and then allow them the opportunity to fulfill that success. I have never met a student who wanted to fail. Hanson and Childs (1998) published the results of a survey given to students in Chicago, Houston, and Norfolk that asked what most concerned them about school. The number one concern (51.77%) was school failure. We have the power to elevate or eliminate that concern. Haberman (1996) says, "Star teachers lead youngsters to believe 'It's you and me against the material.' Quitter and failure teachers lead students to believe, 'It's the material and me against you.'"

A High Level of Support for Achievement

Teachers and students expect quality work; they will not accept anything less. We insult students when we accept mediocre work. Students are given very clear directions about what they must do to be successful, they are given the tools they need in order to make that success possible, and they are given the time to do it right. The expectation is consistent throughout the school; students cannot turn in shoddy work in one classroom and then be expected to do their best in another. A friend of mine who is a powerful math teacher has a sign in her room that says, "I promise to be the best math teacher you have ever had; will you promise to be the best math student you have ever been?" Students who have never before been successful in mathematics are successful in her classroom. It's a matter of attitude.

Kotulak (1996) says,

> Now, thanks to a recent revolution in molecular biology and new imaging techniques, researchers believe that genes, the chemical blueprints of life, establish the framework of the brain, but then the environment takes over and provides the customized finishing touches. They work in tandem. The genes provide the building blocks and the environment acts like an on-the-job foreman providing instructions for final construction.

The environment in which students learn has far-reaching effects on how well and how much they learn. We now know through studies such as those at the University of Alabama that a positive learning environment can actually help elevate IQ scores. Kotulak (1996) goes on to quote Dr. Fredrick Goodwin, the former director of the National Institute of Mental Health (NIMH), who says, "You can't make a 70 IQ person into a 120 IQ person, but you can change their

IQ measure in different ways, perhaps as much as 20 points up or down, based on their environment."

A Sense of Empowerment

All of us feel better about our circumstances when we feel we have some power over what happens to us. Students should have input into the decisions that affect their lives daily. Look at the policies and rules in your school and ask, "How many are necessary, and how many no longer apply but are in place because at some point in the past they were deemed necessary?" In the school that we changed so dramatically, we went to zero rules and rebuilt our list of rules based on the true needs of the students, staff, and community for that time. It was amazing how many rules were on the books simply because, over time, no one had bothered to ask if they were really necessary. Hanson and Childs (1998) say, "In a school with a positive climate, policies encourage and seek a win/win result." Covey (1989) describes win/win as "a frame of mind and heart that constantly seeks mutual benefit in all human interactions. A win/win solution means that all parties feel good about the decision and feel committed to the action plan. Win/win sees life as a cooperative, not a competitive arena." In the classroom, we empower students when we involve them in the class rules and when we give them choices in the assignments. As a matter of fact, anytime we give students choices, we give them power.

In our restructured high school, I saw an amazing application of this principle of giving students choices. We had a nagging problem with discipline; there were fights in the hallway every day. As a matter of fact, the principal at the time said that he watched certain groups of students all the time, waiting for the next fight. Our schedule included a 15-minute activity period designed to give students a chance to go to the library, go by a teacher's room to leave an assignment, or just to give the students a break to have a soft drink and to speak to their friends. Students loved it; we hated it. That was the time when we had the largest number of individual discipline problems. Out of frustration, the principal took the 15-minute break out of the daily schedule.

A group of students, appointed by the general student body, visited the principal to see if there was any way they could get their break time back into the schedule. He told them that he would make a deal with them. He said that as long as there were no fights, no acts of vandalism of school property, and no litter after break or lunch, they could have the break. However, anytime an adult had to break up a fight, anytime there was an act of vandalism, and anytime the hallway was left with debris after break they would lose break for three days. Signs in the hallway informed students whether break was on for the day or not. Over time, there was a dramatic change in the students' behavior; they patrolled between classes and before and after school, and the difference in the school was remarkable. For some students, the 15-minute break was the only time during the school day that they saw their boyfriends or girlfriends and "woe unto" anyone who started a fight and caused the entire school to miss break. One afternoon, I was seated in one of the student's desks waiting for the bell to ring when I heard a commotion outside the door. There were no teachers in sight and, since I was seated at a student desk, no one knew I was there. Two students were getting ready to fight. They were glaring at each other and mouthing off. The tension was high. Before I could get to the hallway, between 10 and 15 students had gotten between the angry students, pushing them back, talking to them, cooling them off—much the way pro athletes do in a game where a penalty would be crucial. This became the norm in that school, and over time discipline problems became minimal.

More On-Ramps

Schools provide plenty of opportunities for students to drop out, physically, mentally, or both. Metaphorically, these are the off-ramps. What we need are more on-ramps to keep students engaged, in school, and on track. Schools can provide more on-ramps by providing more choices in offerings, including not only high-level courses that prepare for higher education, but current, meaningful studies that lead to vocations. Take a hard look at the course offerings and ask some critical questions. What do students really need to know and be able to do in order to have marketable skills? Is there a segment of the school population that is being left out? Could we team up with community colleges and with major universities to provide more opportunities for our students? Why can't students take courses in high school that will help them complete two-year associate degree programs? As a matter of fact, most of those courses could be taught through collaborative efforts with colleges and universities so that students could leave high school with most of the coursework completed. With video-conferencing and distance-learning capabilities, students can complete high school and some college work prior to graduation.

Next, we provide on-ramps when we provide choices within the curriculum that incorporate learning styles and multiple intelligences in the process. Independent projects are a primary opportunity to give students choices for products. The teacher who sets the criteria for the work in the class, yet provides choices within that work, does not diminish the quality of the work, but enhances the depth of the learning by giving students opportunities to bring a variety of products to the learning. Because students learn in different modalities—kinesthetic, auditory, and visual—teachers who teaches with a variety of techniques provides more opportunities for success to their students.

Third, schools provide on-ramps when they lead students to know that if they fail, if they make a mistake, if they break a rule, they can overcome it. I am convinced that we could save quite a few students if they knew that a mistake does not mean there is no hope. While I believe that we need to be accountable for the things we do, I also believe that we must not take away a student's hope that he or she can overcome whatever problem is in the way.

An Advocate for Every Student

I taught in an inner-city high school of 3,000 students in a non–air-conditioned Texas classroom on the third floor. Hardly a day went by without some act of violence, whether it was a student beaten up, a robbery, or slashed tires in the parking lot. I loved my kids; they made tremendous sacrifices just to come to school each day. I learned far more from them than they probably learned from me. One important rule I learned in that environment was that every kid needs an advocate. All kids need to know that someone is looking over their shoulder and knows whether they have been absent too much, whether they are in danger of failure, whether they are on track for graduation, and if they are having problems in the classroom. *Breaking Ranks* (National Association of Secondary School Principals [NASSP], 1996) reminds us,

> During much of this century, reformers sought to shut small schools and herd youngsters into ever-larger schools that styled themselves after the factory model. Experts perceived bigness as a sine qua non of excellence. This paradigm, with its vast array of offerings, represented the epitome of educational progress. But students are not pieces on an assembly line and knowledge is not an inert commodity to pour into vessels like soft-drink syrup in a bottling plant. The impersonal nature of the high school leaves too many youngsters alienated from the learning process.

We know now that the small-school concept is better because it provides the opportunity for teachers and administration to get to know the students personally. Not all of us are in a position to work and learn in small schools, however. In the age of megaschools, there are some creative solutions to providing the small-school experience within the large-school building. Academic teaming, in which teams of teachers are responsible for 100 or fewer students, is one way that we have been able to provide the advocacy needed by students. Under this model, teams meet on a regular weekly, if not daily, basis. Part of the responsibility of the team is to check on the 100 students assigned to see who has been absent too much, who is tardy often, who is a discipline problem, and who is in danger of failure. This team provides support and counseling to these students on an individual basis. The team may meet with other teachers, administrators, support staff, and/or parents on the student's behalf.

Another popular variation of this is the teacher-mentor who is assigned from 20 to 25 students for whom he or she is responsible throughout their school years on that campus. In elementary school, these are often called *homeroom teachers*; at the secondary level, they take on other titles, but the concept is the same. In high school, the teacher-mentor stays with the same students throughout high school and may take on some of the duties of school orientation with the group. These teachers are critical to setting a positive school climate for the students to whom they are assigned.

As we move to a very diverse population, this is especially important in helping to give all students survival skills. Werner and Smith (1992) cite Rutter, who talks about the needs of at-risk children and suggests, "If we want to help vulnerable youngsters we need to focus on the protective processes that bring about changes in life trajectories from risk to adaptation." Rutter includes among them (a) those that reduce the risk impact; (b) those that reduce the likelihood of negative chain reactions; (c) those that promote self-esteem and self-efficacy; and (d) those that open up opportunities. Werner and Smith (1992) explain, "We have seen these processes at work among the resilient children in our study and among those youths that recovered from serious coping problems in young adulthood. They represent the essence of any effective intervention program, whether by professionals or volunteers."

Resiliency in Students

Young children seem to have a tremendous capacity for bouncing back from traumatic and other emotional experiences. That ability is critical to the brain's capacity to function at a quality level. In his book *Inside the Brain*, Ronald Kotulak (1996) talks about the importance of resiliency: "Studies at the University of Chicago on the environmental inputs that may direct the brain down a path of aggression and violence show that the main culprit is stress." Dr. Bruce Perry (1995), a leader in the work at the University of Chicago who has since moved to the Baylor College of Medicine, says,

> Many children are raised in violent, abusive surroundings of which they have no control. The antidote is giving children a sense of self-worth and teaching them they are not helpless. If there's somebody out there who makes you feel like you're special and important, then you can internalize that when you're developing your view of the world.

Perry continues, "When you look at children who come out of terrible environments and do well, you find that someone in their lives somehow instilled in them the attitude that they aren't helpless, that they aren't powerless, that they can do something." Payne (1996) cites the work of Feuerstein and colleagues (1980) with children who came from backgrounds of poverty over generations. Payne says, "For students from generational poverty to learn, a significant relationship must be present." In fact, in the various studies of children who were able to rise above the poverty, all of them could point to a single individual who helped them emotionally.

In their book, *Resiliency in Schools: Making It Happen for Students and Educators*, Henderson and Milstein (2003) list the following characteristics of families, schools, communities, and peer groups that foster resiliency. They

- promote close bonds;
- value and encourage education;
- use high-warmth/low-criticism style of interaction;
- set and enforce clear boundaries (rules, norms, and laws);
- encourage supportive relationships with many caring others;
- promote sharing of responsibilities, service to others, "required helpfulness";
- provide access to resources for basic needs of housing, employment, health care, and recreation;
- express high, realistic expectations for success;
- encourage goal setting and mastery;

- encourage prosocial development of values (like altruism) and life skills (like cooperation);
- provide leadership, decision-making, and other opportunities for meaningful participation;
- appreciate the unique talents of each individual.

Although we cannot ensure that students have that kind of support outside the school, we have tremendous power seeing that they have that support for seven hours each day.

CONCLUSION

As we acknowledge that all learning begins in the self-system of the brain, we must utilize processes in the classroom that help facilitate self-efficacy, positive climate, and adequate challenge so that our students are motivated to learn. Although teachers cannot motivate students directly (motivation comes from within the individual), we can create a climate that nurtures the processes that affect motivation. Namely, we can create an environment that is moderate stress (some stress in the learning prevents boredom), high challenge, realistic in its goals for attainment, and supportive in building the infrastructure to be successful.

Figure 1.3 shows some of the ways that positive environments can be measured and the indicators of success.

Figure 1.3   Indicators of an Environment That Facilitates Learning

Assessment Tool	Indicators of Success
Matrix/rubric	Higher degree of success by students overall
Climate surveys	Results show a high satisfaction with school, low stress level, and a belief that grades, assignments, and assessments are fair and equitable
Overall failure rate	Declining
Attendance rates	Rising
Dropout rates	Low; anything higher than 0 is not acceptable
Discipline referrals	Declining
Course offerings	A wide variety of options that include flexible scheduling where appropriate
Teaching methods	Include visual, tactile, and auditory tools

2

Differentiating With a Variety of Teaching Strategies That Address Different Learning Styles

According to Jensen (1997), about 98% of all new learning enters the brain through the senses—primarily through visual, tactile, and auditory experiences. Taste and smell are also useful avenues for learning, but are not often used in the classroom. Most of us have a preference for how we learn. For example, some of us would rather learn by listening, discussing, and by taking notes. Others of us need to see the information and learn better when there are visual representations of the learning for us to look at while we learn. Still others would rather learn by doing. These are the students who say, "Just give me the information and let me do it."

According to Sprenger (2002), these preferences or strengths may have been brought about through positive experiences. "We use the networks of neurons that solve our problems for us in the easiest and fastest way. As we continue to use those same neurons, the connections become stronger. Therefore if an auditory learner gets positive results from listening and dialoguing, he or she will continue to do so as a preference, and that modality will be strengthened through use." As a matter of fact, there is strong evidence that points to the fact that a so-called slow learner must be retaught in the modality most comfortable for him or her if that student is to be successful (Jensen, 1997).

Schools of the past have relied heavily on lecture as a primary teaching method. Lecture assumes that students learn auditorily, yet through brain research we know that most do not learn that way. Only about 20% of students learn auditorily; the other 80% learn either visually or kinesthetically (Sousa, 1997). While lecture has its place in some courses, it should be used only in short segments . . . 20 minutes or less, depending on the age of the student. It is unrealistic to believe that students who are constantly stimulated by the multimedia world will sit for hours each day passively listening to lectures, taking notes, and preparing for a pencil-and-paper exam without dropping out mentally. Life is not a spectator sport; it is an exercise in active involvement, and education should reflect that active involvement.

Sometimes, educators will say to me, "Well, I learned that way, so my students should also learn that way." That assumption is incorrect because it fails to examine why auditory learning as a single method worked in the past and why it does not today. Remember the old "Nature vs. Nurture" argument about whether our intelligence is based on our environment or on our genetics? The answer is that it is both. We are born into this world with a tremendous capacity to learn and with the wiring to make it happen. Sprenger (2002) says that studies show that 50% to 60% of our intelligence is related to genetics. Then our environment takes over and builds dendrites at an enormous rate.

What does this have to do with lecture? If you had been born in the early part of the last century, your world would have been based largely on listening, reading, and talking. Radio would have been the primary means of gaining national information and entertainment. Reading books was also a way to enlighten and learn—as well as a way to entertainment. If you were privileged, you might have had access to a piano in your home for playing and listening. Your brain became wired to listen, and thus an educational program based on reading and listening was comfortable for you.

Today's students are a part of a multimedia world from birth. They don't just listen; they participate. They don't just sit; they move. Three-year-olds can perform simple computer skills. Why, then, would we think that today's students would be happy learners sitting and listening all day? They aren't restless to make us crazy; their brains are wired to participate. *Breaking Ranks* (NASSP, 1996) echoes this belief in stating, "When possible, students should take an active role in their learning rather than as passive recipients of information passed on by textbooks and by teachers who do little more than lecture." This is a very different type of classroom from the one most often found in schools, where teachers are the imparters of knowledge in a lecture format, while students memorize facts and restate them on paper-and-pencil tests. The transition from a traditional teaching-and-learning format to an active-involvement format takes time and commitment. It is, however, worth it because it is better for students.

In a study led by Marion Diamond (Diamond, Scheibel, Murphy, & Harvey, 1985), baby rats and mature rats were placed in the same cage with rat toys. This is the environment identified by Diamond as enriched and is the environment in which rats in other studies showed brain growth. In this study, the older rats did not allow the baby rats the opportunity to use the rat toys. As a

Figure 2.1   Learning Through the Senses

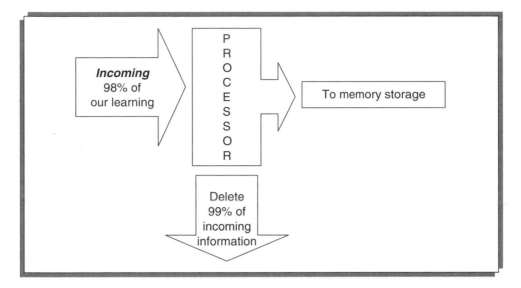

result, the baby rats did not grow dendrites, though the mature rats continued to do so. Diamond concluded that "it isn't enough for students to be in an enriched environment, they need to help create that environment and be active in it."

In order to better understand how learning takes place, we need to examine the modalities through which the majority of our new learning comes. Figure 2.1 identifies the senses or modalities that bring into our brains new learning and new experiences. These make up 98% of the learning. Where does the other 2% come from? It comes from the experiences and prior learning that is extracted from those experiences to make connections to the new learning. The brain filters out about 99% of the incoming stimulus. The upside to that phenomenon is that, if we attended to all of the incoming stimulus, we would be phobic. The downside is that some of the information that we had hoped our students would remember is lost.

AUDITORY LEARNERS

Auditory learners are those who remember best information that they hear and discuss. Information that is auditory is processed and stored in the temporal lobes on the sides of the brain (Jensen, 1998). Auditory students make up about 20% of the classroom. They like lecture, adapt well to it, and tend to be successful in our traditional schools. However, in order for the information to have *personal* meaning to auditory learners, it must be discussed or talked through by the learner: Just hearing and taking notes is not enough. In Chapter 1, I discussed the fact that motivation is based in part on the learner's belief that the information has personal meaning. For these learners, that will only occur after they have been given time to talk it through either to themselves or with each other.

It is important to add that, though these students learn best by hearing, even they grow weary in a straight lecture format. The work of Sousa (1995) and others shows that all of us tend to drop out mentally after 15 or 20 minutes of lecture. In young children, the mental dropout time is significantly less—about 10 minutes.

A good friend of mine was a high school English teacher for many years. We called her the "lecture queen," because not only did she lecture all day, she was good at it. When we began to look at research on attention span and on learning modalities, she decided that it was important to incorporate some other teaching techniques into her classroom so she could reach all of the students. About a month after she started teaching in this new way, she stood in front of the class and said, "Don't you just love the way I am teaching this year?" Because she had moved from teaching junior English to senior English, she had some of the same students in her classroom as the year before. One of those students replied, "No, I hate it." She was crushed. "Why?" The student replied, "Do you remember where I sat last year?" She said that she did and pointed to a chair by the windows at the back of the classroom. The student said,

> What you don't know is that last year I came to class each day, got out my notebook and my textbook, set them up in front of me and went to sleep. You see, the girl behind me took great notes and before each test, she would copy her notes, give them to me, and I would study from her notes. I would come to class, ace your test, and then go back to sleep. But this year, you are making us be an active part of the learning and I am not getting enough sleep.

Sousa (1995, 2001) says that working memory is temporal and deals with information for only a short amount of time before deciding whether or not to discard it. As I stated earlier, the time rate is about 5 to 10 minutes for preadolescents and 10 to 20 minutes for adolescents. Using this information as a guide, secondary teachers should give information for about 15 minutes and then follow it with activities or discussion to reinforce the learning. Elementary teachers should use 7 minutes as their guide. Sousa refers to the teaching segments as prime time. During the first 20 minutes of class, he says, students learn best. New information, information that is of primary importance, should be taught during this time. Figure 2.2 shows how a teacher might use the learning rhythm to enhance student learning.

Sprenger (2002) supplies some additional information about the auditory learner. This learner

1. may look out the window while you are talking but be completely aware of what is being said. Such a learner does not need the visual context of looking at the teacher in order to learn.

2. likes to talk and discuss. Learning does not have meaning until he or she has had a chance to discuss it either with someone else or with himself or herself. As a matter of fact, an auditory learner may move his or her lips while reading.

3. has difficulty sitting for long periods of time without opportunities for verbalization.

Figure 2.2   The Rhythm of Teaching

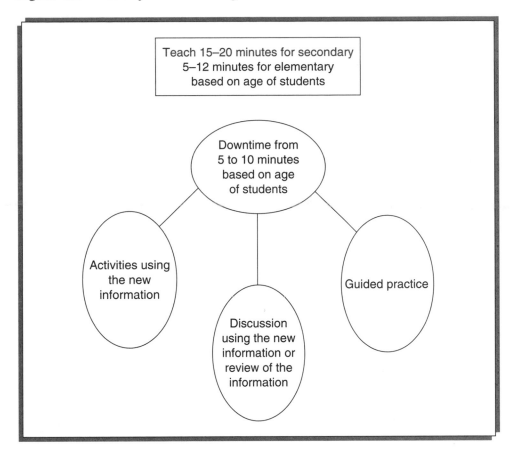

Tileston (2004b) adds that auditory learners

1. like to talk and enjoy activities in which they can talk to their peers or give their opinion,

2. encourage people to laugh,

3. are good storytellers,

4. may show signs of hyperactivity or poor fine motor coordination,

5. usually like listening activities,

6. can memorize easily.

Teaching Auditory Learners

Differentiation does not mean that teachers must teach the same lesson several ways, but rather that a variety of techniques should be used. It also means that for students who do not "get it" the first time, a different approach—one more compatible to that student—should be employed the second time. Jensen (1997) says that slow learners will not "get it" until we teach them in the modality most comfortable for them.

Tileston (2004c) offers the following suggestions for working with auditory learners:

- Use direct instruction, in which the teacher guides the learning through the application of declarative (what students need to know) and procedural (what students can do with the learning) objectives.
- Employ peer tutoring, in which students help each other practice the learning.
- Plan activities that incorporate music.
- Teach using group discussions, brainstorming, and Socratic seminars.
- Assign specific oral activities.
- Verbalize while learning, including self-talk by the teacher and the learner.
- Use cooperative learning activities that provide for student interaction.

VISUAL LEARNERS

The second type of learning modality is *visual*. Visual information is processed and stored in the occipital lobe at the back of the brain. Visual learners are those who need a mental model that they can see. I am convinced that we could raise math scores immediately all over this country if we could find a way to show kids how math works. Since the majority of learners are visual learners, we need to find ways to show them visually how math works. When I work with audiences, I give them the following problem to solve: If five people shake hands with each other, how many handshakes is that? Now, there is a formula that can be applied to find the answer, and the math people in the audience are quick to work the answer out mathematically. But I like to show the answer visually, because it opens up a new world to people in the audience who need to see how the math works. My visual answer is in Figure 2.3. All that is left is to add up the handshakes: 4 + 3 + 2 + 1 + 0 = 10 handshakes.

By the way, the formula is

$$(x)(x-1)/2$$

A more complicated version, such as "One hundred people at the local grocery store shake hands. How many handshakes is that?" is less threatening once we understand how it works.

One of the most effective tools for visual learners is the nonlinguistic organizer, so called because it relies on structure rather than a lot of words to convey meaning. These organizers help students understand and remember difficult concepts, such as sequencing, comparing and contrasting, and classifying. While they are a good teaching strategy for any student, they are important tools for visual students.

The Mid-Continent Regional Education Laboratory (MCREL) looked at studies of the most effective teaching practices for the classroom. They set up a control group to test the studies (meta-analysis) to determine whether current

Figure 2.3   A Visual Math Solution

Let's identify the five people as persons A, B, C, D, and E, respectively.

Person A does not shake hands with himself, so he shakes with

A + B

A + C

A + D

A + E

That is 4 handshakes.

Person B already has shaken hands with A and does not shake hands with himself, so

B + C

B + D

B + E

That's 3 more handshakes.

Person C already has shaken hands with Persons A and B and does not shake hands with himself, so

C + D

C + E

That's 2 more handshakes.

Person D already has shaken hands with persons A, B, C, and does not shake hands with himself, so

D + E

That's 1 handshake.

Person E already has shaken hands with persons A, B, C, and D. He does not shake hands with himself, so that is 0 handshakes.

strategies had any effect on student learning and, if so, how much of an effect. While this work is ongoing, the meta-analysis studies on the use of nonlinguistic organizers are significant. They found that when nonlinguistic organizers were taught and used appropriately, students on average gained percentile points. For example, if a class average is at the 50th percentile and nonlinguistic organizers are incorporated into the learning, the class average can be moved to the 79th percentile. That is the difference between failure (50) and success (79) (Marzano, 2001b).

Nonlinguistic organizers seem to be most effective when incorporated into the learning in the following ways:

1. To help students connect or relate new information to prior knowledge. Because these organizers make abstract ideas more visible, they help students understand and remember concepts that are difficult to visualize otherwise. Young students who have difficulty with abstract concepts can be helped by learning to use a set of visual models that make the abstract concrete. I believe we can raise the scores of students on standardized tests by giving students concrete models to help them perform difficult skills. I am working with a colleague to produce a series of visual models to help students in our area who are struggling on state and national tests. By taking the information that they know and placing it in a concrete model, students are able to transfer abstract thoughts to concrete ideas more easily. Figure 2.4 is an example of a mind map depicting a student's prior knowledge of a topic before the learning. As new information is added, the mind map will add spokes to connect the new knowledge.

2. To help students use information. Nonlinguistic organizers can be used at any time during the learning process, but they are critical in the phase of the lesson in which the teacher wants the students to use the information in some way. This is a time for clarifying ideas for both the student and the teacher—prior to assessment.

3. To introduce a difficult or abstract concept. The old adage, "A picture is worth a thousand words," is absolutely true. Many students have difficulty with logic problems: A matrix is a visual tool that helps make this complex skill more manageable.

4. To assess the learning. Instead of having students list items from the learning, give them a choice to mind map it: "Mind map the key points we discussed in science class today."

5. As part of an individual or group project. Examples might be mind maps, flow charts, or attribute webs. When these tools are used at the application level or above, they can be important products in student projects.

6. To demonstrate creativity. Visual students, once they have been exposed to visual models, have little trouble adding creative and elaborative touches to their models.

7. To depict relationships between facts and concepts. Cause-and-effect, fishbone, and Venn diagrams are examples of mental maps that depict relationships.

Figure 2.4   Mind Map Using Different Shapes

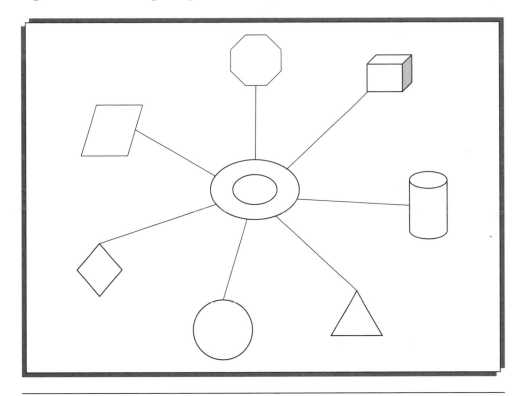

8. To generate and organize ideas for writing. Mind maps and stratification maps are great tools to help students organize their thoughts before writing.

9. To relate new information to prior knowledge.

10. To store and retrieve information. One of my favorite visuals takes vocabulary words—including in other languages—and draws icons to symbolize the meaning of the words. Students who are visual will see the icons as they retrieve the information from their brains.

11. To assess student thinking and learning.

12. To depict relationships between facts and concepts.

Tileston (2004c) adds that visual learners

- have difficulty understanding oral directions,
- may have difficulty remembering names,
- enjoy looking at books or drawing pictures,
- watch the speakers face,

- like to work puzzles,
- notice small details,
- like for the teacher to use visuals when talking,
- like to use nonlinguistic organizers.

Teaching Visual Learners

Some ideas for working with visual learners include the following:

- Use visuals when teaching. Remember, these students need to "see" the learning for it to make sense to the self-system.
- Directly teach students to use visual organizers.
- Show students the patterns in the learning.

Anytime we can help visual learners see the information, we help them process it toward long-term memory.

KINESTHETIC LEARNERS

The third learning modality is *kinesthetic.* Kinesthetic information is stored at the top of the brain in the motor cortex until permanently learned, and then it is stored in the cerebellum, the area below the occipital lobe (Jensen, 1998). Kinesthetic learners learn best through movement and touching. In the previous handshake exercise (Figure 2.3), kinesthetic learners would solve the problem by physically shaking hands with four other people and counting the handshakes. Provide opportunities for your class to go outside, to go on field trips, or to role-play. In addition, and whenever possible, provide opportunities for them to move around in the classroom, to change groups, or just to stand. The old adage that we think better on our feet is absolutely true. When we stand, we increase the flow of fluids to the brain and we do learn better. Take advantage of that in the classroom by having students stand to give answers or to discuss with each other.

Sprenger (2002) adds the following information about kinesthetic learners:

1. Kinesthetic learners need hands-on activities. The learning will not have meaning until they have an opportunity to do something with it.

2. These learners respond to physical closeness and physical rewards, such as a "pat on the back."

3. Kinesthetic learners may become discipline problems in a traditional setting unless they are given the opportunity for movement.

4. These learners may slump down in their seats (the comfort of the room is important to them) or they may wiggle a great deal in traditional classrooms.

Tileston (2004c) adds the following characteristics about kinesthetic learners: They

1. need the opportunity to be mobile;

2. want to feel, smell, and taste everything;

3. may want to touch their neighbor as well;

4. usually have good motor skills, may be athletic;

5. like to take things apart to see how they work;

6. may appear immature for their age group;

7. may be hyperactive learners.

Teaching Kinesthetic Learners

Providing opportunities for movement in the classroom can make a tremendous difference in the behavior and learning for these students. Tileston (2004c) offers the following suggestions for meeting the needs of these students:

- Use a hands-on approach to learning.
- Provide opportunities to move.
- Use simulations when appropriate.
- Bring in music, art, and manipulatives.
- Break up lecture so that it is in manageable chunks (a good rule is to talk to a student only for the number of minutes based on his or her age—for a 10-year-old, 10 minutes).
- Use discovery learning when appropriate.
- Use such techniques as discussion groups or cooperative learning so that these students have an opportunity to move about and to talk with their peers.

CONCLUSION

Although we all record information using all three modalities, most of us have a preference for one of the modalities. Sousa (1995) says teachers need to understand that students with different sensory preferences will behave differently during learning and that teachers tend to teach the way they learn. That explains, in part, why so many students have trouble learning from one teacher, but may learn easily from another. Behavior that has been interpreted to mean the student was not interested in the learning or did not want to learn may, in fact, have only been an indication of inappropriate teaching techniques

Figure 2.5   Indicators of a Classroom in Which a Variety of Teaching Strategies Are
Used to Address Different Learning Styles

Evaluation Tool	Indicators of Success
Teaching time	Follows the rhythm of the brain with 15 to 20 minutes of instruction followed by 10 minutes in which the students do something with the learning for secondary students, or, for elementary students, instruction in approximately 10-minute segments followed by opportunities to work with the new learning
Lesson plans	Indicate opportunities for students to stand and move, to go on field trips, and to explore the environment
Lesson plans	Indicate a variety of visual tools are used
Student projects	Indicate choices that include visual, kinesthetic, and auditory learning
Teaching practices	All reteaching is done in the preferred modality of the learner

or a classroom where only one modality was valued. The classroom that is
enriched with teaching techniques from all three modalities and in which
new information is given in 15- to 20-minute segments for secondary and 7- to
10-minute segments for elementary students, with time for processing in
between, will be a place where quality learning is possible.

Figure 2.5 shows common indicators of success for this teaching strategy.

Strategies That Help Students Make Connections From Prior Learning and Experiences to New Learning Across Disciplines

Teachers should not assume that transfer will automatically occur after students acquire a sufficient base of information. Significant and efficient transfer occurs only if we teach to achieve it.

—David Sousa, *How the Brain Learns* (1995)

The human brain seems to be wired to seek connections. Anytime we are given new information, there is an effort within the structure of the brain to attach that new information to knowledge or experiences already in place. Thus, it makes sense that the more we can help students make connections between what they already know and the new knowledge, we are more apt to provide positive learning experiences.

In the meta-analysis studies conducted through MCREL, building connections prior to the learning had a high effect size on student learning. Marzano (1998) calls this strategy "direct schema activation." In the studies conducted, the average achievement score was raised by 27 percentile points representing an effect size of 0.75. This means that, in a classroom in which the average student is at the 50th percentile range, the class average can be moved above the 70th percentile range just by correctly employing this technique in the teaching process.

Sousa (1995, 2001) refers to the brain's process of making connections between old and new learning as *transfer*. The strength of this process is dependent on two factors. First, the effect of the past learning on the new learning and, second, the degree to which the new learning will be useful in the future. When new information is introduced to working memory, a search is conducted in long-term memory for past learning that connects to the new learning. When those connections are made successfully, Sousa (1995, 2001) says greater achievement is possible. He refers to this as *positive transfer*. Negative transfer occurs when past learning interferes with new learning. Sousa uses the example of learning to drive a standard shift car after driving only an automatic shift car in the past. The skill of leaving the left foot on the floor of the car for driving an automatic shift car can be a hindrance if transferred to the standard shift car where the left foot must be moved onto the clutch for shifting.

What if there are no prior experiences and knowledge on the subject to be taught? We have said that the brain is a seeker of connections. We have all had the experience of being in a room where something is being discussed about which we have no knowledge. There is confusion and frustration while we work to find a connection or hook for the new information. For some students, this is a daily occurrence. What this means in the classroom is that we cannot assume that students come to us with the structures already in place to learn new material. We must first establish what they know and understand and, where there are no previous connections, supply them for the student.

Bruer (1993) makes a strong case for the relevance of prior knowledge: "A good teacher will consciously capture attention and relate it to prior knowledge because how we understand and remember new material depends on what we already know. Our brains make sense of what we experience by actively connecting it with prior knowledge." Pyle and Andre (1986) echo these findings: "What a student acquires from instruction is determined as much by what the student already knows as by the nature of the instruction. Using previous knowledge to elaborate upon the presented information facilitates its transfer into long term memory." When the student relates new information to old information already in long-term memory, the student is more likely to learn and remember the new information. Prior to the introduction of new material, we must first find out if the prerequisite knowledge is there.

Sousa (1995, 2001) identifies four factors originally identified by Madeline Hunter that influence the rate and degree of retrieval. They include *similarity, critical attributes, association/context,* and *degree of original learning.* Let's look at the four factors and how classroom teachers might use those factors to help students make connections.

STRATEGIES **29**
THAT MAKE
CONNECTIONS
FROM PRIOR
LEARNING
TO NEW

ASSOCIATION

Sousa defines *association* as events, actions, or feelings that are learned together so that the recall of one prompts the recall of the other. In my book *Strategies for Teaching Differently* (Walker, 1998), I refer to this part of the lesson as *personal connection*, because it is the process of providing a hook or connection that makes the learning personal. Personal or association connection is based on the association of past experience, past knowledge, or, in the event that there are no past experiences, on the associations that we create. It is the process of going from the known to the unknown.

This is probably the most common way that teachers help students bridge the new-learning gap. We want to find some experience or information that the student already has in long-term memory to which we can connect the new information. This is why teachers often refer back to previous lessons if the information to be studied requires the prerequisite of the information from the previous lesson. When there is no previous lesson from which to draw, we can create the hook with personal experiences the students may have had. If we can draw from personal experiences, especially those with emotional ties, we have a greater chance of making the new information relevant to the learner.

As mentioned in Chapter 1, the brain ties itself to strong emotions. The amygdala, found in the forebrain, is responsible for encoding emotional messages and bonding them to the learning for long-term storage. Emotion is so strong in the brain that it takes priority over everything else. We are therefore more likely to remember something when we have an emotional tie to it. I often ask audiences to think back to the youngest age they can remember. The events they remember are usually either very happy or traumatic. Both are strong emotional ties. Emotions can also play a negative effect on making connections. Students who have always experienced problems with math will come to math class with negative transfer even before the lessons begin.

When drawing on past experiences to which students may have emotional ties to introduce new information, the following examples might be used. Whisler and Williams (1990) give this example: In elementary school, prior to reading *Earrings* by Judith Viorst, ask, "Have you ever wanted to do something that your parents said you could not because you weren't old enough?" In middle school, prior to a lesson on the Boston Tea Party, ask, "Have you ever encountered a rule that you felt was unfair to you in some way? Did you try to talk to someone about it? Did they listen?"

Personal or association connection is the piece that gives ownership to the learning process. Prior to a lesson on estimation, ask, "Have you ever seen those contests where you must guess how many jelly beans are in a jar?" By giving the problem personal application, we create ownership. All of us are more interested in things to which we feel personal attachment: "What kind of strategy would you use to win the contest?" Prediction is another way we help create ownership to the learning by using students' natural curiosity to hook them into the learning. This is the marketing to which I referred earlier. We want to know about tomorrow's weather so we can plan accordingly, so we wait diligently during the news. Just before commercial break, the newscaster says,

"Big changes coming in the weather, stay tuned after our commercial break for the details." They have us hooked so we will stay around for the details. This is a great technique to hook kids into reading and learning material that otherwise might not seem exciting. Fitzgerald (1996) gives these examples of using prediction to hook kids into the learning:

> A science teacher is introducing a unit on electro-magnetic radiation so he holds an electric razor up to an electro-magnetic radiation meter to set off the warning light. (An indication of radiation above the recommended level for human tissue.) A speech teacher shows clips from the Kennedy-Nixon debate and asks what skills or lack thereof will influence the outcome.

Elementary teachers often use this technique by showing pictures or giving information prior to reading a story to pique the kids' interest. A secondary teacher says, "In *Romeo and Juliet* there is going to be a major fight between two gangs tonight. What do you think will happen?" Sousa (1995, 2001) says that these hooks or connections should be given to students a day, even a week, before the learning to give them thinking time to get interested in the subject.

Personal or association connection is the link between previous knowledge and new knowledge: "Last week, we talked about slope and how it is used in the real world to figure the dimensions of wheelchair ramps. Today, we are going to measure wheelchair ramps around the building. Before we do that, let's review what the law says about the dimensions of these ramps and how we determine slope." Not only are we linking knowledge, but we have also heightened the need to know with the fact that the students are going to do something with the information.

Figure 3.1 is an association tool that I use to help students make connections between old learning and experiences to the new learning. The K represents the old "Knowledge, skills and experiences" that students have with the subject. The N represents information that students will "Need to know" about the topic. This is another way of setting personal goals for the learning. The L represents "Learned information" that is completed after studying the topic. The importance of this metacognitive activity is to help students synthesize what they have learned. Jensen (1998) says that we do not know something until we are convinced that we know it. Until then, it is just meaningless information. Have you ever been to an all-day conference in which you were bombarded with a great deal of new information that you were sure you would remember and use only to find when you got back to your school that it was a jumble? The H represents "How did you learn the information?" The "how" of the process is important because it helps bridge the gap between the borrowed opinions of others to the personalized and warranted opinions discovered by the learner.

Before introducing a new unit, I ask my students to brainstorm ideas or information that they already know about the new subject. Figure 3.2 is a graphic organizer that I use to help students put the information into an organized structure to help them see the connections.

STRATEGIES **31**
THAT MAKE
CONNECTIONS
FROM PRIOR
LEARNING
TO NEW

Figure 3.1   KNLH Chart

Know	Need to Know	Learned	How Learned

Categories 1.

2.

3.

4.

5.

Figure 3.2   Indicators of a Classroom in Which Curriculum Facilitates Transfer
From Prior Learning Experiences to New Learning and Across Disciplines

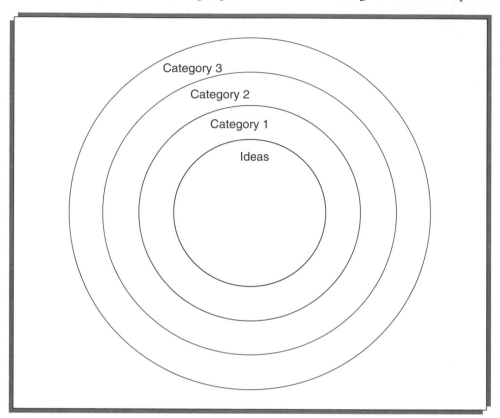

Those thoughts and information gleaned from the brainstorming session
are written in the center circle of the organizer. For example, for our unit on
world hunger, I ask them to list everything they already know about world
hunger in the inner circle of Figure 3.2. Then, I ask them to look at the information that they have listed and to place any information that would be related
to transportation in the Category 1 circle, anything that would be related to
politics in the Category 2 circle, anything that would be related to medical conditions in the Category 3 circle, and so on. By asking students not only to recall
information, but also to put it into categories, I am providing word associations
early in the learning to help them retrieve information when they need it. This
exercise also provides the teacher with important information: What do
students already know about this subject that doesn't need to be retaught and
what misinformation do they have that needs to be corrected up front before
they place it in long-term memory?

A word of caution on any technique to introduce a lesson: Be sure that
incorrect information is corrected immediately so that it does not become a part
of long-term memory. We tend to remember those things that are discussed in
the first 20 minutes of class, so it is critical that we make the most of that time
in getting important facts on the table correctly.

STRATEGIES **33**
THAT MAKE
CONNECTIONS
FROM PRIOR
LEARNING
TO NEW

After the students have made their lists and we have made a class master list from their information, I give them a lead-in or emotional hook to create interest. I might say, "In this country, we produce enough food each year for every man, woman, and child in the world to have 2,500 calories each day, so why do we have world hunger?" By giving them an interesting tidbit of information about world hunger—that it is not a matter of food production, which most of them thought—I hook them into the learning. Then, I lead them to ask questions. This approach is not unlike the evening news programs that give us a small amount of information just before commercial break to keep us watching. I ask, "So, what would you like to know about world hunger?" From the information that they provide, I make a "Want to know" list. During the unit on world hunger, we will refer back to this list often so that students can see that their questions and concerns are being answered. By doing this, I am giving them a *personal connection* or association to the learning.

Association or personal connection can also be the bridge between disciplines. There are many natural links between disciplines, and we need to point these out to students. We cannot assume that they will naturally get the relationship between the study of World War II in history and the study of the John Hersey's novel *Hiroshima* in English class. In our restructured high school, we had a wedding to marry math to science and English to history. Teachers worked across disciplines to realign the curriculum so that those natural connections could take place at the same time. We did not change *what* we taught, just *when* we taught it. As we became more cognizant of what our colleagues were teaching, the benefits were transferred to our students. Departments made joint assignments so that, instead of several fragmented projects, the projects moved across disciplines. Because students were working on fewer individual projects, they could present more complex, in-depth projects. In elementary school, we have a natural vehicle for doing this, since the schedule allows the same teacher to teach across disciplines. As schools become more advanced in this technique and as student e-mail is introduced into classrooms, students will have opportunities to create projects that not only go across disciplines, but across grade levels as well.

SIMILARITY

Sousa (1995, 2001) defines *similarity* as the process of transfer "generated by the similarity of the situation in which something is being learned and the situation to which that learning may transfer." Thus, behavior in one environment tends to transfer to other environments that are similar. He uses the example of pilots who are trained in simulators and then transfer that experience to the actual plane.

In my book *Strategies for Teaching Differently* (Walker, 1998), I use similarity when students do not have exact prior knowledge or experience to connect to the new learning. In this instance, I relate the new information to something similar that they already understand personally. Jacoby (1991) uses a demonstration lesson on immigration that showcases this concept very well. Before beginning the unit, she asks, "What would have to happen in your life to cause you to pick up everything you can carry and move to a place where you know no one and a place about which you know very little?" Because students tend to give her the same kinds of answers, she then asks, "What would have to happen economically in this country to make you leave? In the religious arena? Politically? Medically?" That way, when she gets around to talking about why people get in leaky boats to risk their lives to emigrate, students have a connection for understanding.

CRITICAL ATTRIBUTES

Sousa (1995, 2001) identifies *critical attributes* as "characteristics that make one idea unique from all others." *Unique* is the key word here, since it is important that students identify how things are different so that retrieval will be easier. Sousa says that long-term memory files new information into a network with similar information, but, when it retrieves it, memory looks for differences so that the right piece of information is retrieved. He uses the example that we recognize our best friend not by the attributes that make him or her like everyone else, but by features that make him or her unique. We have all had the experience of looking for someone in a crowd. For a moment, everyone looks alike; they all have faces, bodies, and hair. The way we find the person we are seeking is in looking for features unique to that person, such as black hair, tall body, and sharp chin.

Since the brain already has stored patterns and structures from previous learning and experiences, teachers build on those patterns for similar information that is new. This technique makes use of the brain's search for patterns for understanding. Patterns might be categories, such as those given in the example on immigration, or rhymes and letter games, such as those in mnemonic devices. Graphic models are great tools to help visual students create attributes. Use mind maps or organization tables with key concepts to help students form patterns for the new learnings. Since 80% of the learners in the classroom learn either visually or kinesthetically (Jensen, 1998), it is important to include visual models to help connect the learning.

CONTEXT AND DEGREE
OF ORIGINAL LEARNING

Sousa (1995, 2001) says that, when the original learning was well learned and accurate, new learning will be more powerful. This factor is a great argument for teaching a concept for mastery, not just to cover the subject. Many teachers are frustrated by the amount of material that is required by state, national, or local policies without regard to whether the students actually learn it. We can only hope that as brain research is understood, schools will take another look at not only how information is taught, but also at the time frame in which it is taught.

STRATEGIES **35**
THAT MAKE
CONNECTIONS
FROM PRIOR
LEARNING
TO NEW

CONCLUSION

Eric Jensen (1998) says, "The brain thrives on meaning, not random information." We should not assume that students come to us with the necessary structures in place to make the necessary connections to new information and across disciplines. We must first find out what they know, what misinformation they have about the subject, and, where no structures exist, create structures for the new information. When we do this, we help students "get it" from the very beginning. Although it takes some class time to do this, it may very well save time in the long run, because reteaching will not be needed to the degree that it would be without it.

Figure 3.3 shows indicators for success for this chapter.

Figure 3.3   Indicators of a Classroom in Which Curriculum Facilitates Transfer From Prior Learning Experiences to New Learning and Across Disciplines

Assessment Tools	Indicators of Success
Lesson plans	Indicates that students are provided opportunities to create connections to the new learning prior at the beginning of new lessons or units. Where prior knowledge and experience do not exist, the teacher provides that information before going to the new material.

Teaching for Long-Term Memory Is a Primary Goal

Through current research we can, for the first time in history, work smarter, not just harder.

—Donna Walker Tileston, *What Every Teacher Should Know About Learning, Memory, and the Brain* (2004)

Have you ever crammed for a test, aced the test, and then two weeks later encountered a question from the test and said, "What in the world is that?" We have all experienced the frustration of teaching a great lesson only to find out weeks later that the students remember very little of what was taught. Schools have often emphasized the fact that students must learn material for "the test" rather than learning because it has relevance to student needs beyond the test. While the brain is willing to put information into short-term memory for a short-term goal, it needs more incentive for remembering for the long term.

Chapter 2 discussed three of the modalities through which we receive incoming information. They are the visual, which is stored in the occipital lobe at the back of the brain; the auditory, which is processed by and stored in the temporal lobes on the sides of the brain near the ears; and the kinesthetic, which is stored at the top of the brain in the motor cortex and later in the cerebellum. Once the information enters the brain through the various modalities, it is held in the association cortex until it is tossed out, sent to working memory, or sent back to long-term memory (Sprenger, 1999). Once new learning has been registered through the perceptual or sensory register in the brain stem, it moves to (a) temporary memory, which is made up of short-term memory and which is in turn an extension of the perceptual register, and (b) working memory, where processing occurs (Sousa, 1995, 2001). Short-term memory holds information for only about 30 seconds while it decides whether to toss it or move it along. Sousa uses the example of looking up a phone number and retaining it only long enough to make the phone call. If the number is needed later, it will have to be looked up in the telephone directory again. Because the number was not perceived to be important enough to be put into long-term memory, the brain tossed it after the number was called.

Working memory is the place where information is processed. At this point, the information has our attention while we mull it over. Working memory can handle only a few chunks of information at one time. Sousa says that preschool infants deal with only two items of information at once, whereas preadolescents deal with three to seven items, with the average being five. From adolescence through adulthood, seven to nine chunks are handled at one time, with seven being the average (Sousa, 1995, 2001). Jensen (1998) uses a similar guide. He says that infants hold about one item of information in working memory at a time, with the number increasing by one every other year of life to adolescence, where seven to nine items are held in working memory. There is a difference of opinion on how long information remains in working memory before being tossed out or sent to long-term memory, but it seems to be about 5 to 10 minutes for preadolescent children and 10 to 20 minutes for adolescents and adults. Sousa says that after 20 minutes, if something is not done with it, the information will probably be dropped from working memory.

If the learner is ever to recall this information in the future, it must be stored in long-term memory. A simple guide for how information enters and is stored includes the following point: About 98% of all new information enters the brain through the senses, and we have five senses—taste, smell, hearing, sight, and touch.

The brain holds information in working memory while it decides whether to send it on to long-term memory. In order to understand long-term memory, we must look at the brain's storage system. The number of memory pathways in the brain are probably many more than we have yet discovered. Even of those about which we know, there is discussion about the number. Some researchers say that there are five, while others say that there are only three. Those in the latter class of thinking believe that the emotional lane is actually a part of all of the lanes and thus not a separate pathway. Some believe that the automatic pathway, is actually not a separate memory system but rather a part of the procedural pathway. For the purposes of this book, I will discuss the five memory pathways. I use the analogy of a five-drawer file cabinet that assists with retrieval in the brain (see Figure 4.1).

Each drawer represents a different storage system. The systems are *semantic*, which holds information from words; *episodic*, which deals with locations; *procedural*, which deals with processes; *automatic*, which deals with conditioned response; and *emotional*, which takes precedence over all other types of

Figure 4.1 The Brain's Retrieval System

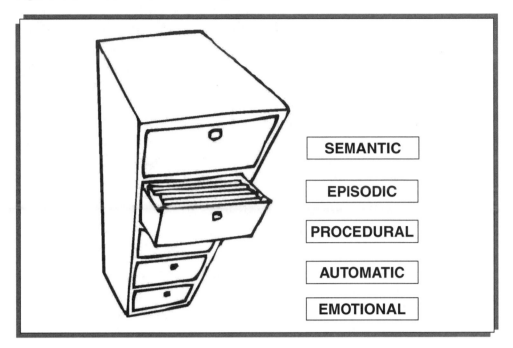

memory (Jensen, 1998). Some researchers, such as Jensen (1998), only include three storage systems: semantic, episodic, and automatic. Jensen includes the procedural with the automatic system. Others, such as Sprenger (1999) and Tileston (2000), include all five of the systems. The truth is that there are probably more than five—these are only the systems that we know at this time.

Let's look at each of these drawers in our memory file cabinet individually.

SEMANTIC MEMORY

Semantic memory holds the information that was learned from words. New information enters through the brain stem and passes through the thalamus to the hippocampus, where a search is conducted for matching information. If a connection is made, the information will go to working memory (Jensen, 1998). Semantic memory goes to the prefrontal cortex where it is rehearsed and where processing takes place. Semantic memory either has to be rehearsed a sufficient number of times for the learner to remember it or it has to have a hook or attachment so that the learner can retrieve it from its memory pathway. On test day, have you ever had students who say, "I know I know that, but I can't remember." The truth is that they probably do have it in the memory pathway, but it was not stored so that it is easily retrieved.

Semantic memory is the most difficult to retrieve from long-term storage. Facts, dates, and vocabulary are difficult to memorize without sufficient time, repetition, and hooks to help the learner remember the stored information. According to Jensen (1997), "The brain is poorly designed for remembering print and text copy. Information embedded in content is usually learned, or attempted to be learned, through rote tactics and by following list-like formats."

Two hooks or attachments are important in ensuring that the brain stores the information in long-term memory. These three hooks boost the process. The first hook for semantic memory is relevance or meaning. The question becomes, "What does this have to do with the world in which I live?" We have all had students who ask, "When are we ever going to use this?" Students ask not to drive us crazy, but because they really need to know in order to make the learning meaningful. Several years ago, I attended one of William Glasser's workshops. Glasser said that he could teach anyone anything as long as he could make it relevant. After all, he said, very young children learn one of the hardest things to learn—they learn a language—and no one stands in front of them with flash cards (Glasser, 1994). They learn it because it is relevant to their world. If we can give the information relevance in the classroom, there is a good chance that it will be remembered. Keefe (1997) says we can create meaning by modeling, by giving examples from experience, and through artificial meaning, such as mnemonic devices.

The second hook for semantic memory is patterns created by prior knowledge or experience. Sousa (1995, 2001) calls this "making sense" of the information. Is there already a pattern in place into which the new information can fit? Do I have prior knowledge or prior experience with which to hook onto the new information? Students will be able to learn and remember statistics more easily if they have a prior knowledge of algebra. Jensen (1995) cites the work of Renate Nummela Caine, which concludes, "The ability to make meaningful sense out of countless bits of data is critical to understanding and motivation." Jensen suggests that, prior to the learning, we create a global overview, give oral previews, or post mind maps to help form the patterns for the instruction. During the learning, we should allow students to discuss the topic and to create models, mind maps, or pictures. After finishing a topic, we should give the learners the opportunity to evaluate it, discuss relevance, or demonstrate patterning with models, plays, or teachings. For example, Pat Jacoby (1991) introduces a unit on immigration by asking students what would cause them to leave this country. Next, she asks what would have to happen in this country politically for them to leave. Economically? In the religious arena? By doing that, she provides a hook or pattern for the learning that is about to take place. When students get around to the economic, religious, and political reasons why people emigrate, they have prior learning to create a hook for the new learning. During the lesson, provide opportunities for students to use the information in such visuals as mind maps or through written diagrams. Jensen (1998) says that the semantic memory pathway requires repetition of the learning and needs to be stimulated by associations, comparisons, and similarities. The immigration example makes use of associations in a concrete way.

Of the two hooks, relevance and patterns, Sousa (1995, 2001) says the most important is relevance. He goes on to say that most classrooms spend the majority of lesson time on making sense of the new information and little time on giving it relevance. By shifting the emphasis to relevance, students would more likely retain the learning at a higher rate.

Tileston (2004c) recommends the following tactics to teachers to help students store and retrieve semantic information:

- Use nonlinguistic organizers, such as the mind map, to help students organize and remember the learning.

- Use peer teaching, in which students are paired with another student to review information. One of the ways to do this is to stop at intervals and ask students to tell each other what they remember from the information they have just been given.

- Put the information into manageable chunks by classifying or categorizing long lists.

- Use questioning strategies, such as Socratic Questioning, to help students process the information.

- Make your room reflect the unit you are studying. Elementary teachers do a good job of this, but somewhere between middle school and high school this techniques becomes lost. Just changing the room to reflect each unit helps the brain sort the information based on visuals present in the room when the information was learned.

- Wear hats or use symbols with the learning to help students remember. For example, I use picture frames when we are talking about frames of reference. Sometimes, when my students cannot remember, just saying, "Remember, it was on the blue picture frame" will help trigger the memory.

- Use mnemonics or stories to weave the information into memory. On a recent news show, students participating in the national memory contest were asked how they remember all to the trivia and data they are given to memorize. One student said, "We weave a story around it to help us remember."

- Use music. Music leaves such a strong emotional impression on each of us. Bring in music to introduce and reinforce learning in the classroom.

- Use linguistic organizers to help your students with the learning. For example, to help students remember the various math concepts that you will study, you might provide an organizer, such as the one in Figure 4.2.

EPISODIC MEMORY

The second memory drawer in our file cabinet is *episodic*. Episodic memory is based on context and location (Where were you when you learned the material or in what context did you learn?) Sprenger (1999) uses the example of tending to remember where we were at the time of a traumatic event, such as the assassination of John F. Kennedy. According to her, students who learn information in one room and are tested in another tend to underperform. This has

Figure 4.2 Matrix for Math Class

Math Unit	Formulas	Explanation	Example of Use

tremendous implications for giving standardized tests to students in the room in which they prepared for the test.

Sprenger (1999) also talks about the invisible information within a room. For example, if a bulletin board in a room has information about the multiplication tables and the information is taken down while students take a test on multiplication, students tend to look at the blank bulletin board to help recall facts. Kay Toliver (1995), an outstanding teacher who has had so much success with teaching the at-risk children of Harlem, uses props to help students with learning. For a math lesson on multiplication, she comes to class with placards across the front and back of her torso that are a replica of a box of raisins. Her students worked with multiplication using raisins. What a great tool to help students when it comes time for recall on multiplication facts! Sprenger (1999) uses fact sheets printed on different colors of paper, depending on the subject of the fact sheets. When students are having trouble with recall, she mentions the color of the paper that contained the facts.

One example of the way in which episodic memory is used might be that of watching television when the commercial for some type of medication comes on. That reminds us that we need to call the pharmacy to renew a prescription. We get up to go to the bedroom to make the call. On the way, a family member asks a question that we answer but by the time that we get to the bedroom, we can't remember why we are there. We go back to the couch in front of the television and at the next commercial we suddenly remember why we went to the bedroom. Our memory was triggered by the suggestion from the television and then by the place we were sitting when we received the cue. Once we are distracted, we lose the cue, but sitting back on the couch helps re-cue us to go call the pharmacy.

Tileston (2004c) provides the following suggestions for teachers to help students make better use of the episodic memory system:

1. Put information up so that it is visually accessible to the learners who need visuals to learn well. For English language learners, visuals are critical to their learning because they have limited semantic (language) acquisition strategies.

2. Color code units or use symbols, especially if there is a great deal of vocabulary involved.

3. Use graphic (nonlinguistic) organizers to help students "see" the learning and teach students to develop graphic organizers of their own for learning.

4. Change the room arrangement prior to a new unit. This technique affects context ("Remember we talked about that information when you were all seated facing the windows").

5. Use symbols and/or costumes to help students separate the learning. I use frames (frames of reference) when studying pollution. One group of students has a frame that says "politician," another group has a frame that says "new parent," another group has a frame that says "factory owner." Each group must talk about pollution according to the "frame of reference" they have been given. The frame serves as a *context* for the learning.

It is important to note here that Eric Jensen cites recent research in his workshops that provides evidence to support the fact that when we test students in the same room in which they learned the information, they do better on the test. In light of what we know about the episodic memory system, this makes sense.

PROCEDURAL MEMORY

The third drawer of our memory file cabinet is for *procedural* memory. Procedural memory is actually stored in the cerebellum, which is responsible for muscle coordination (Sousa, 1995, 2001). Processes such as driving a car are stored in this part of the brain. Rehearsal plays an important part in this memory. For example, I will not be able to remember how to drive a car unless I have practiced the process. If we want students to perform an operation easily, we must have them rehearse or perform the material often enough that it becomes procedural. One of Steven Covey's (1989) rules is called the *28-Day Rule*. Basically, the rule says that if you repeat a behavior for 28 days, it becomes internalized. Often used in changing behaviors, this rule draws on procedural memory to change negative thinking into positive by repetition. Jensen (1998) says that we enhance procedural memory through hands-on activities, manipulatives, role playing, and physical skills.

This system may be the strongest in terms of remembering. To make better use of this system, Tileston (2004c) suggests that we add movement to the learning. When we do, we tend to give it great strength in terms of storage and retrieval. Some teaching strategies that seem to reinforce this system include the following:

1. Role playing

2. Drama

3. Choral readings

4. Projects

5. Hands-on activities

6. Manipulatives

7. Debates

8. Group activities

AUTOMATIC OR CONDITIONED RESPONSE

The fourth drawer of the memory file cabinet is *automatic* or *conditioned response.* Automatic memory is triggered by stimuli. Any learning that has become automatic is stored in this drawer. For example, the ability to read is found in this drawer, but the ability to understand the reading is not: Other memory drawers, such as the semantic memory, deal with meaning. The alphabet, multiplication tables, and so on can also be found in the automatic drawer. When the information is tedious or when it is not used often, such as vocabulary words that are not used in everyday conversation, mnemonic devices can act as triggers. Jensen (1998) says that if we can weave a story around the information, it is more likely that students will remember.

I was doing a workshop in California and a man in my audience told me that he uses the following tool to help teach his students the parts of the body in his anatomy class. He has made up an elaborate story about a man who gets caught in a snow bank, and through the story he uses the names of the parts of the body to tell the story. For example, the man who tries to pull the car out of the snow is the *pullman*; he is doing the most work because he is pulling instead of pushing. He is like the *pulmonary artery*. He said that what was once difficult for students to remember has now become easy through this technique.

EMOTIONAL MEMORY

The fifth drawer of the memory file cabinet is the most powerful of all the memory drawers: *emotion.* The brain tends to remember those things to which it has an emotional attachment. Jensen (1995) says, "The stronger the emotion, the more the meaning. Emotional experiences 'code' our learning as important." Think back to the youngest age you can remember. If you are like most of us, your earliest remembrance is probably either very happy or traumatic in some way. That is because the brain remembers vivid emotional experiences. My earliest remembrance was when I was four years old. I thought it would be fun to hide from my parents, so I went outside and hid in a corner of our house. It was all fun until I saw my parents go by looking for me, and they were not having fun—they were very upset. I later learned that they had the whole neighborhood out looking for me. Jensen says we tend to remember our highest highs and our lowest lows: "This applies across all areas of life: the best and the worst vacations, meals, dates, jobs, weather and so on." Emotions can and do influence retention.

Jensen (1995) goes on to say,

> Make a purposeful strategy to engage positive emotions within the learner. Without it, the learner may not code the material learned as important. Long, continuous lectures and predictable lessons are the least likely to be remembered. Utilize the following: enthusiasm, drama, role-playing, quiz shows, music, debates, larger projects, guest speakers, creative controversy, adventures, impactful rituals and celebrations.

CONCLUSION

In a classroom in which a conscious effort is being made to ensure that students are putting the information into long-term memory and will be able to retrieve it when needed, teachers will provide tools to help facilitate the process. Emotion, relevance, and concrete models that assist students to move random facts to a concrete form will be an ongoing part of the teaching process. Teachers will employ techniques that pique student interest and that motivate students to know more. Lessons will be dynamic and of high interest, and will employ emotion where appropriate. Students will see the application to real life so that they buy into the learning from the start. The teacher, as role model, will demonstrate a love for learning that will translate to students. In this environment, students and learning will thrive.

Figure 4.3 shows the indicators for success for the strategies discussed in this chapter.

Figure 4.3   Indicators of a Classroom in Which Teaching for Long-Term Memory Is a Primary Goal

Assessment Tool	Indicators of Success
Lesson plans	Indicate that teachers employ techniques to pique student interest in the learning
Lesson plans and observations	Indicate that lessons are dynamic, of high interest, and presented in such a way that students are actively involved
Students' tasks and projects	Indicate use of emotion, relevance, and high-interest materials
Student assessment	Includes opportunities for reflection and self-assessment

5

Constructing Knowledge Through Higher-Level Thinking Processes

Knowing the facts and doing well on tests of knowledge does not mean that we understand.

—Benjamin Bloom, *Taxonomy of Educational Objectives* (1956)

We live in an age of tremendous information that changes rapidly; if students are to be successful in life they must move beyond factual input to the processes involved in higher-level thinking, such as problem solving, decision making, experimental inquiry, and investigation. We want to move students from the simple to the complex. I am not suggesting here that we give students more work or even that the work we give be more difficult in terms of their ability to complete the assignment. Both of those examples are an exercise in bringing about frustration and low motivation within our students. Students today need complexity. These are students who can surf the Internet with ease and who can discuss a wide variety of universal topics. Simply giving them rote facts to memorize and give back on a test is boring.

Sousa (1995, 2001) warns that there is a significant difference between complexity and difficulty. Complexity refers to the thought processes that the brain uses to deal with information. Each level of Bloom's Taxonomy (Bloom, 1976) represents a different level of complexity. Difficulty, however, refers to the amount of effort expended within a level of complexity. A learner might expend a great deal of energy on difficulty while working at a low level of complexity. Sousa gives the example of requiring a student to name the states and their capitals in order of their admission to the Union. This example takes place on the lowest level of Bloom's Taxonomy, the knowledge level, but requires some effort on the part of the student. Knowledge is considered to be low-level skill because the student does not even need to understand the information in order to process the question; the student merely needs to be able to provide facts from a book.

While there is certainly nothing wrong with the above-mentioned assignment, students who are never allowed to go beyond this level or who expend so much effort at the low levels that they do not have time for the higher levels of thought are robbed of the opportunity to grow mentally. Teachers mistakenly think that slower students cannot work in the higher levels of the taxonomy, although studies by Bloom (1976) show that the opposite is true. When these students are given only the critical attributes of the learning, without extraneous information to sort, they are able to perform at a more complex level. Sousa (1995, 2001) concludes that teachers can get slower students to be successful at the higher levels of Bloom's Taxonomy if they review the curriculum, remove extraneous information and topics of least importance, and provide time for practice at the higher levels.

Marzano (1992) described the context of higher-level thinking as "extending and refining knowledge." This type of thinking should be a part of every unit of study. Students who learn in this way give personal meaning to the learning. They are literally taking the information provided by others and giving it personal context through what they do with the new information. Marzano says, "In social studies class, for example, students might compare democracy and dictatorship to discover new distinctions between them. In a science class, students might make deductions about whales based on known characteristics of mammals to refine and extend their knowledge about mammals and whales."

There are three basic reasons for using higher-order thinking in the daily instruction of students. They are the need for *information literacy*, the need for *quality processes*, and the need for *quality products*. These three reasons involve processes that require critical and creative thought, which requires students to look at information frontward, backward, and in ways never viewed before (see Figure 5.1).

INFORMATION LITERACY

Resnick and Resnick (1997) identify literacy as rational thinking. Literacy involves the ability to analyze information, extrapolate key points, generate a hypothesis, draw conclusions, and find viable solutions. In Chapter 1, I discussed the need for students to create their own goals for the learning. This is not only brain friendly, it also leads to higher-level thinking. Wiggins and McTighe (1998) suggest that the work must be purposeful from the student's

Figure 5.1   Using Higher-Level Thinking Skills

I. *Critical thinking* is the ability to analyze, to create and use objective criteria, and to evaluate data. Critical thinking includes the following:
   A. Inductive Thinking Skills
      - Cause and effect
      - Open-ended problems
      - Analogy
      - Making inferences
      - Identifying relevance
      - Relationships
      - Problem solving
   B. Deductive Thinking Skills
      - Using logic
      - Understanding contradiction
      - Syllogisms
      - Spatial problems
   C. Evaluative Thinking Skills
      - Fact and opinion
      - Credibility of a source
      - Identifying central issues and problems
      - Recognizing underlying assumptions
      - Detecting bias, stereotypes, and clichés
      - Evaluating hypothesis
      - Classifying data
      - Predicting consequences
      - Sequencing
      - Decision-making skills
      - Recognizing propaganda
      - Similarities and differences
      - Evaluating arguments

II. *Creative thinking* is the ability to use complex thinking structures to produce new and original ideas. Creative thinking includes the following tools:
   - Attributes
   - Fluency
   - Flexibility
   - Originality
   - Elaboration
   - Synthesis

III. *Problem solving* is the ability to utilize complex thinking to solve real problems. The steps may include the following:
   - Identifying the problem
   - Analyzing the problem
   - Formulating a hypothesis
   - Formulating appropriate questions
   - Generating ideas
   - Developing alternative solutions
   - Determining the best solution
   - Applying the solution
   - Monitoring and evaluating the solution
   - Drawing conclusions

point of view: "Regardless of how abstract the key ideas are or the student's degree of naiveté about the subject, we as educators must embody the goals in known, practical tasks and standards that the student can understand from the beginning of the unit." Thus, we lead students into higher-level thinking from the beginning by requiring that they create personal goals that include the following:

1. What will I understand by the end of the unit or lesson? What will that understanding look like?

2. How will I be assessed? How will I know that I have learned?

3. What resources will I use? Do I know how to use them?

4. What is my plan for learning? What will I do if my plan is not working?

5. Why is this work important to me personally? Why is it important to others?

It is important to note that higher-level thinking by students does not mean that all of the learning is abstract. Students must be directly taught how to set goals, how to plan, and how to adjust their plans when things are not going well. We cannot think in the abstract if we do not have the basic structures (scaffolding) for that thinking. Wiggins and McTighe (1998) have a great example of this. They explain that if we are lost and stop at a gas station for directions, we want concrete, clear directions. We don't want the attendant to ask Socratic questions such as, "Why do you want to go where you are going? How did you decide to go there?" We need directions, not rhetoric.

Let's examine some of the tools that lead to higher-level thinking once those basic structures or scaffolding are in place. Marzano (1992) provides eight tools that help lead students to extend and refine knowledge. These tools are the gatekeepers to higher levels of thought.

Comparison

Comparison is a way in which we identify the similarities and the differences between two or more things. To do this, the students must be able to identify the attributes of each of the things that he or she is comparing. For example, if a student is comparing fiction and nonfiction, the student needs to know what makes a book fiction and what makes it nonfiction before he or she can compare. These characteristics are called *attributes*. Fiction has certain attributes that make the selection fiction rather than nonfiction. For example, fiction contains content and/or people that are made up by the writer. The main purpose of a work of fiction is to tell a story. Nonfiction is based on factual information. Its main purpose is usually to relay information to the reader. Being able to compare and contrast is a necessary skill if students are going to be successful on state tests. Don't believe me? Look at the benchmarks for your state test. For example, almost every state has a standard that involves students'

Figure 5.2   Attribute Comparison Chart for Nouns and Verbs

Noun	Attributes	Verb
Nouns may change spelling for plural form.	SPELLING	Verbs change spelling for the third-person singular form.
Proper nouns are capitalized no matter where they fall in the sentence.	USE OF CAPITALS	Verbs are only capitalized if they begin the sentence.
Nouns name a person, a place, or a thing.	WHAT THEY NAME	Verbs name actions.
Nouns do not change tense.	USE OF TENSE	Verbs change tense to show present, future, or past.

Figure 5.3   Attribute Comparison Chart for Comparing Several Criteria

Parallelogram	Quadrilateral	Rectangle	Square	Trapezoid	Attributes
Has two sets of parallel sides	May have parallel sides—two or more	Has two sets of parallel sides	Has two sets of parallel sides	Has only one pair of parallel sides	PARALLEL SIDES
May or may not have right angles	May or may not have right angles	Has four right angles	Has four right angles		RIGHT ANGLES
Some but not all parallelograms have two equal sides	Has four sides	Has four sides	Has four sides		FOUR SIDES
	May be a quadrilateral				PARALLELOGRAM
May be a parallelogram					QUADRILATERAL

knowledge of the various genres of writing. The benchmark expects the student to know not only the differences between fiction and nonfiction but also the differences among tall tales, fantasy, and so forth.

An effective way to teach comparing strategies is with nonlinguistic organizers, such as the compare-and-contrast chart shown in Figure 5.2. In this figure, students are comparing only two things—nouns and verbs. Notice that students must identify how they are different according to given attributes that are critical to identifying what makes them different. When comparing more than two things, the chart in Figure 5.3 is a useful tool. In this chart, students are comparing four-sided shapes.

Figure 5.4   Venn Diagram Compare/Contrast for a Rectangle and a Square

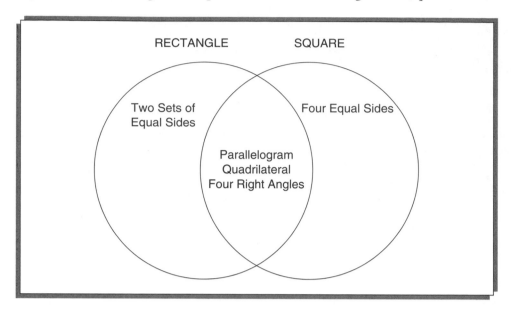

Classification

Students who can classify understand how to use attributes to place things into categories. They also understand that things may go into more than one category. Venn diagrams are often used when classifying items. In Figure 5.3, we identified the attributes of four-sided shapes. Figure 5.4 utilizes a Venn diagram to compare and contrast two of those shapes—a square and a rectangle. Note that the left side of the diagram shows the attributes that are only true of rectangles; the right side identifies these attributes for squares. The center circle identifies common attributes. Here are the definitions, from Parks and Black (1992), of each of the shapes to help you as you examine the Venn diagram:

- Parallelogram: a quadrilateral with two sets of parallel sides
- Quadrilateral: any closed, four-sided shape
- Rectangle: a parallelogram with four right angles
- Square: a rectangle with four equal sides
- Trapezoid: a quadrilateral with only one pair of parallel sides

If your students have difficulty with Venn diagrams (which are showing up on state and national tests more frequently), begin with a comparing chart and then move them to Venn diagrams.

Marzano (1992) uses the following questions to assist students in using classification:

- Into what groups could you organize these things?
- What are the rules for membership in each group?
- What are the defining characteristics of each group?"

Induction

Induction is the ability to take what is known and predict what is not known. It is an important higher-level skill to assist students to make informed decisions about their world not only at this time, but throughout life. We cannot teach students everything that they will have to know in life. What we can do is teach them these higher-order skills that can be employed to specific facts throughout life. After studying the patterns involved in earthquakes and the major earthquakes that have occurred so far, students might infer when and where the next earthquake in California might take place.

Deduction

Deduction differs from induction in that induction is based on possible conclusions drawn by observation and facts; deduction is based on rules and principles that lead to absolutes. Induction deals with the unknown; deduction deals with what is known based on the principles involved. For example, in Fibonacci math, the sequence 1, 2, 3, 5, 8 . . . is followed by 13. This is known because the rule is that the two numbers prior to the new number add up to the new number. Thus, we can deduce that the next number in the sequence is 13. Deduction only works if the premises are true. For example, if the rule of Fibonacci math is not as stated, then the deduction is incorrect. Where inductions are *probable*, they are not *absolute*; deductions are absolute. Deductive arguments can be categorical, conditional, or linear (Klenk, 1983) Syllogisms are an example of categorical deduction in which there are two premises and a conclusion that is a result of the premises. Syllogisms are usually written like this:

All A are B.

All B are C.

Therefore, all A are C.

Error Analysis

The ability to determine fallacy in thinking and to evaluate our own thinking and then the thinking of others is a skill worth developing. Because this involves personal evaluation, it is not necessarily a popular skill. Marzano (1992) recommends the following questions to aid with error analysis:

- What are the errors in reasoning in this information?
- How is this information misleading?
- How can it be corrected or improved?

Constructing Support

Building support for ideas is a critical part of life. Students who learn the principles involved in skillfully being able to glean proof and support will have an important life skill as well as a tool that helps extend their knowledge. Persuasive writing is based on this ability. Marzano (1992) places constructing support into the four categories, or "four appeals," developed by Kinneavy (1991):

1. Appealing Through Personality. Using this appeal, the speaker or writer has as his or her goal to be liked. This is usually done through personal information about the speaker or writer in the form of stories and anecdotes.

2. Appealing Through Accepted Beliefs and Traditions. The writer or speaker uses basic truths that are held by the audience to make a point. For example, "In Texas, this is the way we do things."

3. Appealing Through Rhetoric. By using language and gestures, the writer or speaker appeals to the audience.

4. Appealing Through Logic. The speaker or writer uses evidence, elaboration, and examples to win over the audience to his or her way of thinking. For example, "In this country, we produce enough food each year for every man, woman, and child in the world to have more than 2,500 calories per day. Why, then, do we have world hunger?"

Abstracting or Pattern Building

In Chapter 1, I discussed the fact that the brain likes and seeks patterns. The ability to create and understand patterns is an important skill in constructing meaning. Students who are adept at this skill look for underlying causes and for ways that one phenomenon relates to another. A student falls asleep in his third-period class every day: What is the underlying reason behind his need for sleep at that time each day? I once had a student who was lethargic and unproductive every Monday in class. Investigations into the problem proved that he was being abused on the weekends.

The second part to this type of thinking is the ability to see new patterns based on patterns that already exist. Linda Booth Sweeney's *When a Butterfly Sneezes* (2001) is built around patterns that occur in literature that can be applied to the real world. Ray Choiniere and David Keirsey, in *Presidential Temperament* (1992), ask the question, "If I know the mood of the country and the personality types of the presidential candidates, can I make an accurate prediction (based on past experiences) about who will win the election?"

Analyzing Perspectives

Analyzing perspectives is the ability of the learner to view events and information from a perspective other than his or her own. Marzano (1992) suggests the following questions to analyze perspectives:

- Why would someone consider this to be good (or bad or neutral)?
- What is the reasoning behind their perspective?
- What is an alternative perspective and what is the reasoning behind it?"

Those were Marzano's eight tools. Additional higher-order thinking skills that are important to student understanding and refinement of knowledge follow.

Critical Thinking

Critical thinking is the ability to think at a complex level and to use analysis and evaluation processes. Critical thinking involves inductive thinking skills, such as recognizing relationships, analyzing open-ended problems, determining cause and effect, making inferences, and extrapolating relevant data. Deductive thinking skills are also involved in critical thinking; they include solving spatial problems, using logic, constructing syllogisms, and distinguishing fact from opinion. Other critical thinking skills include detecting bias, evaluating, and comparing and contrasting.

Creative Thinking

Creative thinking is complex thinking that produces new and original ideas. Paul Torrence (1966) is considered by many to be the father of creative thinking. He developed a model around four attributes:

1. Fluency: the ability to generate many ideas. An example would be to ask students to brainstorm what they know about world hunger.

2. Flexibility: the ability to generate many different ideas. An example would be to ask students to brainstorm what they know about world hunger in regard to medical aspects, economic aspects, political aspects, and so on.

3. Originality: the ability to generate unique ideas.

4. Elaboration: the ability to generate many details. Students who have difficulty on the writing portion of state and national tests usually receive low scores because they cannot elaborate.

Problem Solving

Problem solving uses sequential skills to solve complex problems and incorporates the ability to see and analyze underlying causes. These skills are necessary because students must have higher-order thinking skills in order to perform quality processes. O'Tuel and Bullard (1993) say that "process is as important as product in education. Note that the words 'as important' not 'more important than' were used. This is because students need an information base upon which to build."

We all tend to be creative when we are children, but sometimes in elementary school that creativity takes a nosedive. Major corporations have put lots of money into retraining their people to be creative. Creativity is essential in a world where change is happening so quickly. If business, industry, education, or any other institution is to survive and remain marketable, it must involve the processes of creative and critical thinking. Joel Barker (1992), in his book *Future Edge,* says the element that will make our students marketable in this new century is not quality—that will be the minimum expectation—it is creativity.

Curriculum must include opportunities for students to utilize higher-order thinking skills, such as the ability to use both convergent and divergent processes, to think critically, and to investigate real-world solutions to complex problems.

Newmann and Wehlage (1993) say, "Knowledge is thin or superficial when it does not deal with significant concepts of a topic or discipline—for example when students have a trivial understanding of important concepts or when they have only a surface acquaintance with their meaning." The reason for this is usually an attempt to cover quantities of information:

> Knowledge is deep or thick when it concerns the central ideas of a topic or discipline. For students, knowledge is deep when they make clear distinctions, develop arguments, solve problems, construct explanations, and otherwise work with relatively complex understanding. Depth is produced, in part, by covering fewer topics in systemic and connected ways. (Newmann & Wehlage, 1993)

In addition, higher-order thinking leads students to create quality products. How many of us have assigned independent studies to classes only to receive finished products that are far less than our expectations. Time is too precious a commodity in schools to waste in producing finished products that are low level and below the abilities of our students. Finished products should reflect the higher-order thinking skills of quality processes. At the highest level, the products should benefit not only the student, but others as well. If we use the rationale of Bloom's Taxonomy, for example, it is possible to provide students with high-quality expectations for finished products by providing clear parameters for the finished product. Teachers must set parameters that ensure quality, then must teach the process skills and must set benchmarks so that there are no surprises when the finished product is turned in. Figure 5.5 shows a process for assigning student projects.

Simply put, the levels of Bloom's Taxonomy are as follows:

1. Knowledge level: to know something and be able to recite it back. Verbs that indicate assignments at this level include *list, outline, recall, locate,* and *describe.*

2. Comprehension level: to understand something and to be able to explain it. Verbs that indicate assignments at this level include *interpret, demonstrate, explain,* and *infer.*

3. Application level: the ability to use information and ideas. Verbs that indicate assignments at this level include *apply, classify, organize, solve,* and *use.*

Figure 5.5   Bloom's Taxonomy

Bloom's Level	Verb	Process	Product

4. Synthesis level: the ability to take something apart and put it back together in new and unusual ways. Verbs that indicate assignments at this level include *combine, construct, generate,* and *reorganize.*

5. Analysis level: the ability to break something down into manageable parts. Words that indicate assignments at this level include *differentiate, diagram, infer, simplify,* and *syllogize.*

6. Evaluation: the ability to judge something. Verbs that indicate assignments at this level include *appraise, determine, evaluate, weigh,* and *rank.*

Remember, Bloom's Taxonomy does not get more difficult as we move up it—we can add difficulty at any level; rather, it becomes more complex.

To use the taxonomy, a teacher would determine the level or levels of Bloom's in which the product would fall, use the appropriate verb to distinguish the taxonomic level, identify a process to produce the product, and then identify an appropriate product. Students should be given choices of products. This follows the philosophy of constructivist thinking, which holds that we learn based on schema or patterns already established and that we interpret new stimulus and information based on that schema. O'Tuel and Bullard (1993) give the example of a large dog in a yard. One person might approach the dog with no fear because he has a similar dog at home, while another might hide behind a tree because of a negative experience with another dog. Because we do react differently to new information and because we want to encourage creativity, students should be given some choices in the way learning is approached. If we want quality, however, we must set the parameters.

The teacher might provide a list of possibilities from which students choose their projects. The value of the projects might differ according to the level of difficulty. See Figure 5.6 for examples.

Figure 5.6   Examples of Formulas for Student Projects

Bloom's Level	Verb	Process	Product
Knowledge	*list*	the freedoms included in the Bill of Rights	as a newspaper advertisement to encourage patriotism
Comprehension	*explain*	slope to your class	in such a way that a student new to class would understand
Application	*draw*	illustrate how to identify and classify parallelograms	flowchart
Synthesis	*create*	using the elements of short story writing and information relating to compromises, property, and the aftermath	an original short story about the talks at Yalta
Analysis	*analyze*	the organizational structure of two works of art from the Renaissance period	compare-and-contrast chart
Evaluation	*judge*	the underlying reasons for World War II	a rank-order chart with narrative

CONCLUSION

When higher-order thinking skills are a part of the learning, students use more complex thinking processes. Critical thinking, creative thinking, and problem solving should be encouraged and rewarded. The teacher should filter the material to be studied so that low-level and extraneous information are kept at a minimum to allow time for processing more complex skills. To the extent possible, student products and assessments should be at the analysis level or above. Inductive thinking skills, such as distinguishing cause and effect and making inferences, should be a part of the lesson plans, and students should be provided opportunities to use deductive thinking skills, such as logic and syllogistic thinking. All students should have the opportunity to work at higher levels, not just students identified as fast learners. When we do this, we raise the floor of achievement, making our way to raising the roof.

Figure 5.7 shows the indicators that will be present when higher-order thinking skills are a part of the learning.

Figure 5.7   Indicators of a Classroom in Which Higher-Level Thinking Skills Are
Integrated Into the Lesson

Assessment Tool	Indicators of Success
Student products	Indicate that critical thinking skills, creative thinking skills, and problem-solving skills are encouraged and rewarded
Student products and assessments	Are at the analysis level of Bloom's Taxonomy and above
Lesson plans	Indicate inductive thinking skills, such as cause and effect
Lesson plans	Indicate deductive thinking skills, such as logic and syllogisms
Student products	Indicate an understanding of the vocabulary of higher-order thinking skills
Student products	Indicate that students can perform the steps of complex problem solving

6

Collaborative Learning Is an Integral Part of the Classroom

High schools continue to go about their business in ways that sometimes bear startling resemblance to the flawed practices of the past. Students pursue their education largely in traditional classroom settings, taught by teachers who stand before row upon row of desks. Mostly, these teachers lecture at students, whose main participation in class is limited to terse answers to fact-seeking questions.

—National Association of
Secondary School Principals,
Breaking Ranks (1996)

Collaboration is more than just working together in groups; it is the whole communication process in the classroom. How does the teacher communicate with students in regard to the information to be learned and how it is to be assessed? How do students communicate with the teacher and with each other? What is the role of the parent? Is the communication one-way, two-way, or multiple? Is it in the form of written, oral, tactile, or computer-generated communication?

In the studies reported by Diamond (1998) in which rats were placed in environments enriched with rat toys and then compared with rats placed in impoverished environments with no rat toys, it was found that rats with toys had more dendritic branches than those without toys. What is significant in terms of the need for collaboration is another phase of her study. In this experiment, one rat was placed in a cage with rat toys (enriched environment) and another rat was placed in a cage alone, without rat toys (impoverished environment). A control group of three rats was placed in a larger cage without rat toys. Although the single rat with rat toys grew more dendritic branches than the single rat with no rat toys, the rats that grew the most dendritic branches were the three rats placed together, even though they did not have toys. This would suggest that we learn more in environments where we are with others.

To be successful in the job market, students must be able to articulate what they know and to listen to the ideas and opinions of others. Students practice cooperative and collaborative learning strategies to help solidify what they have learned and to practice the learning so that when it is time for individual assessment, the learning is in long-term memory. Sizer (cited in O'Neil, 1995) says,

> The real world demands collaboration, the collective solving of problems . . . [and] learning to get along, to function effectively in a group is essential. Evidence and experience also strongly suggest that an individual's personal learning is enhanced by collaborative effort. The act of sharing ideas, of having to put one's own views clearly to others, of finding defensible compromises and conclusions, is in itself educative.

How can we ever expect students to learn the higher-level social task of criticizing ideas, not people, if they have not learned the basic task of collaborating effectively with others?

The Secretary's Commission on Achieving Necessary Skills (SCANS) report (U.S. Department of Labor, 1991) was an eye-opener at the time it was released, because it said that while it is important for students to know reading, mathematics, and writing skills, one of the most important marketable skills that we can give students is the ability to work with other people. That information should have been no surprise since we have known for years that the primary reason why people lose jobs is not incompetence but the inability to get along with others. Students need classroom opportunities to work with everyone else in the classroom at some point in time. Even very young children need social skills. It is one thing to know information; it is another dimension to be able to explain that information to someone else. Add to that the ability to do quality problem solving with small groups and you have a winning combination.

When we were working on research for our restructured school, one of our consultants visited with members of business and industry to ask firsthand what the important skills were that we should be teaching students. The answer was overwhelming that we should be teaching social and collaborative skills. One oil company said that, when prospective employees come in for an interview, the company brings them in small groups to the office. There, they are given a problem to solve. They are given a choice: They can work together on the solution or they can work in cubicles to solve the problem alone. What the prospective employees do not know is if they choose to work alone, they will not be called back for a second interview. The Association of Supervision and

Curriculum Development (ASCD) said in its 1999 yearbook, "The process of learning has passed from simple self-organization to collaborative, interpersonal, social problem-solving activity dependent on conversation, practical, meaningful involvement, and real world experience and application."

Four primary communications are important to making collaborative learning significant in the classroom. First, *communication between the teacher and students* is crucial. In Chapter 1, the significance of classroom environment and the power of a positive climate were presented. The teacher sets the tone for the classroom through verbal and nonverbal communication. Not only is what is said to students important, but the tone and body movements are important as well. Jensen (1998) says that high stress and threat in the classroom impair brain cells. He goes on to say, "Threat also changes the body's chemistry and impacts learning." If students are made to believe that, no matter what they do, they cannot be successful in the classroom, threat exists. In Chapter 1, evidence was presented that the success of our students can be dramatically raised just by saying to them that we will not let them fail and then backing that up with actions. Jensen (1998) provides these additional examples of threat in the classroom:

1. Anything that embarrasses students

2. Unrealistic deadlines

3. A student's inability to speak a language

4. Uncomfortable classroom cultures

5. A bully in the hallway

6. Inappropriate learning styles

7. Out-of-class factors, such as a fight with family members

8. Threat of being sent to the principal

When threat exists, the brain operates in survival mode, and while we can learn in that mode, we do so at the expense of higher-order thinking.

Once a positive climate has been established, the teacher must communicate expectations verbally and in writing. Why both? Eighty percent of the students in the classroom do not learn auditorily. Expectations include classroom rules as well as learning expectations. Prior to any assignment in which students will be assessed, they should be told verbally and in writing what they have to do to be successful—and that should be followed to the letter. When we tell students in advance what it takes to be successful, we take away the "gotchas." There are no surprises: Students know in advance how they will be assessed, whether through a rubric or through some other written communication. These rubrics should be specific. When we make them specific, we help level the playing field so that everyone starts with the same opportunity for success.

Teachers must also set benchmarks, which include frequent intervals to check for student understanding. These should be interspersed within the class day or class period. Sousa (1995, 2001) says that assessment for a grade should

Figure 6.1   Ticket Out the Door

Three things I have learned are . . .

1. _____

_____

_____

2. _____

_____

_____

3. _____

_____

_____

One thing I do not understand is . . .

_____

_____

_____

_____

not come until 24 hours after learning, because we cannot be sure that the information is in long-term memory until at least that amount of time has passed. Benchmarks, however, refer to making sure the students understand—not to assessment for grades.

Effective communication between students and teacher also requires what I call *cruise control*. As a teacher, I cruise the room while my students are working so that I know on an ongoing basis who is off task, who doesn't understand, and who is in danger of failing. When one of these factors is present, I can intervene immediately. Another tool for doing this is a tool I call the *ticket out the door*. In *Strategies for Teaching Differently* (Walker, 1998), I provide examples of this technique. Basically, in order to get out the door when the bell rings, students must give me a ticket that has assigned questions. An example of a ticket out the door is shown in Figure 6.1.

For very young students, I use faces—happy faces, sad faces, and neutral faces. Students give me a face that signals how they feel about the day. This is a nonthreatening way for students to let me know if all is not going well and a tool for early intervention before it is too late.

Last, the teacher must begin to take on the role of coach, leader, or guide in the classroom to stir the students by dynamic, interesting presentations of the learning that allow them to participate actively. The teacher cannot continue to be the lecturer with the students as passive listeners. Students today come from a sound-bite world that constantly bombards the senses. They will not—they cannot—sit all day as passive listeners. Jensen (1998) says, "Today's teachers must think of themselves as a catalyst for learning, not a live, breathing textbook. Schools simply must have greater roles, like creating motivated, thinking, responsible, and productive citizens for the next century."

The second necessary communication link is *student-to-student communication.* Jensen (1998) says,

> Our brain cannot be good at everything, therefore, it selects over time that which will ensure its survival. As a species, the human brain has evolved to use language as our primary means for communication. This may partly explain why groups, teams and cooperative learning benefit our understanding and application of new concepts; group work requires us to communicate with each other. Through this process, learning seems to be enhanced.

We learn best when we teach something to someone else. As a teacher, when did you know your subject best? Probably when you taught it to someone else. We need to make use of this powerful teaching technique by giving students opportunities to tell about the learning.

Students also need the opportunity to work with other people—not just their best friends. Social skills, group interaction skills, conversation skills, and group problem-solving skills are some of the highest-level skills we can give to our students. These abilities may have more to do with their success in life than the academic skills we give them. They certainly have a great deal to do with their finding satisfying and rewarding relationships—both personal and collegial. For teachers who have not attempted group activities in the past but are convinced it is worth trying, I offer the following guidelines:

1. Start small—begin by letting students work in pairs for a short amount of time. The ideal time to use this would be after presenting information for 15 to 20 minutes, during the 10 minutes of downtime. Have students discuss what has been said, formulate questions about the new material, or use the information in some way. Not only does this produce social skills, but it also helps solidify the new learning.

2. The first few times that students are put into small groups, use familiar material. A unit you have never taught before is not a good time to try group work for the first time.

3. Make sure that any assigned group work is meaningful. Students know when it is busy work and will react accordingly.

4. Time all activities and stick to the time schedule. Allow only enough time for the groups to do the work effectively—push the envelope a little. If you tell students they have 8 minutes to complete an activity and you give them 15, they will not take the time limit seriously the next time.

5. Tell students up front why they are working in small groups. Tell them it is an important real-world skill and you want them to be highly successful in whatever they do. Tell them it is a privilege to get to work with other people instead of doing all the work alone. Tell them about synergy.

6. Sign up for instruction in cooperative learning techniques. You will learn a great deal about how to set up groups and how to manage them.

The third essential communication is *communication with parents.* Letters, notes, e-mail, phone calls, parent conferences, and group meetings are essential to maintaining a positive climate. In our restructured school, we had a VIP (Very Important Parents) Committee. This committee helped create an open-door policy for parents and was the catalyst for setting up parent meetings—both individual and group. Parents were welcome in the school and were encouraged to sit in classrooms at any time. Our only requirement was that the parents sign up in advance with our VIP chairperson. This last requirement was for safety, so that we always knew who was in our building. An interesting thing happens when parents are in classrooms and hallways: Discipline problems are diminished. An added benefit is that those parents become advocates in the community. We never held staff development sessions that parents were not invited to attend. I believe that is why we were able to make such radical changes in such a short amount of time. Anytime someone in the community said, "I don't know what they are doing at that school," there was someone who had been to the meetings, to the school, or in the training who could speak for us.

Fourth, *communication between the teacher and other staff members* is important to the overall climate of the building. Teachers need the opportunity to work with each other just as students do. It is difficult to set a classroom climate that is positive if the climate outside the classroom is negative. Unless the administration is supportive, teachers will have a difficult time creating a collaborative environment. I have known situations where this was done, but the individual teachers spent many exhausting and frustrating days and nights to make it happen.

In our restructured school, teachers met daily in small teams to discuss a variety of topics. This time was built into the school day. Each team of teachers was responsible for 100 students. They were responsible for seeing whether any of them were absent too often, having discipline problems, or in danger of failure. Students with problems were called in to meet with the whole team. Teachers also discussed assignments for the week.

It is difficult to understand why some nights kids have no homework and other nights they are stressed over an unrealistic amount of work. Communication can help solve that problem. Teachers who meet daily can discuss upcoming assignments and work together on making them more evenly spaced. This is also the way to integrate learning. These are so many natural ways to connect one subject to another—*natural* meaning that the connection is already there, that it does not have to be forced. In our restructured school, the more integrations we made, the more we found. As a result, math, science, English, and social studies became naturally aligned.

CONCLUSION

Where multiple communication is present in the classroom, interaction will be evident. Students will be actively discussing with the teacher and with each other. Newmann and Wehlage (1993) say that this interaction should include "indicators of higher-order thinking such as making distinctions, applying ideas, forming generalizations, raising questions, and not just reporting experiences, facts, definitions or procedures."

In addition, in a multiple-communication classroom, the teacher will act as a catalyst to the learning, not as the living textbook. Newmann and Wehlage (1993) add, "Sharing of ideas is evident in exchanges that use not completely scripted or controlled (as in a teacher-led recitation). Questions are asked in complete sentences and responses are made to the comments of other speakers." Students will be provided numerous opportunities to work together to practice the learning, to develop concepts, to discuss ideas, and to produce quality products. Mutual respect will be evident in the verbal and nonverbal communication of the teacher and the students. Students will be actively engaged, not passive receivers of the information. Moreover, risk taking will be encouraged and supported. The teachers as well as the students will be risk takers with the learning. Social skills will be a part of the learning and the assessment process. SCANS (U.S. Department of Labor, 1991) puts collaborative skills right up there with math and reading, so they should be given importance in the classroom, not just because they are a skill for the marketplace, but also because they are a skill for life. Projects and assignments should clearly indicate that effective collaboration has taken place.

Teachers and administration should have active, ongoing communication with parents as an integral part of the process. In this multiply communicative school, every day is open house, for an open-door policy will exist that allows parents to visit the classroom and to communicate with teachers and staff whenever needed.

Figure 6.2 shows the indicators that will be present when multiple communication channels are present in the classroom.

Figure 6.2   Indicators of a Classroom in Which Collaboration Is an Integral Part of
the Learning

Assessment Tool	Indicators of Success
Observations	Indicate that interaction is a part of the classroom and that it follows the precepts of Newmann and Wehlage (1993), who say that interaction should include higher-order thinking skills, such as making distinctions, applying ideas, forming generalizations, raising questions, and not just reporting experiences, facts, definitions, or procedures
Observations	Indicate that the teacher acts as a catalyst to the learning, not as a living textbook
Lesson plans and observations	Indicate that students are provided numerous opportunities to work together to practice the learning, to develop concepts, to discuss ideas, and to produce quality products
Observations	Mutual respect will be evident in the verbal and nonverbal communication of the teacher and the students
Observations, student products	Students will be actively engaged, not passive receivers of the information
Observations, student assessment	There is an expectation that students will master social skills
Projects and assignments	Clearly indicate that effective collaboration has taken place
Climate surveys	Indicate that teachers and administration have active, ongoing communication
Parent surveys	Indicate that parents feel that they are a part of the process; an open-door policy exists to allow parents to visit the classroom and to communicate with teachers and staff

Bridging the Gap Between All Learners, Regardless of Race, Socioeconomic Status, Sex, or Creed

As the economy, resources, and affluence of the city have moved to the suburbs, we have been left with many large cities whose inner-city area is a myriad of crumbling buildings, graffiti, and the poor who cannot afford to leave. Add to that a struggling economy and the lack of resources available, and we have an educational system that, despite its best efforts, cannot provide equal access to success.

—Donna Walker Tileston, *What Every Teacher Should Know About Working With Diverse Learners* (2004)

The time has come to quit assuming that all students come to us with the scaffolding in place to be successful in school. They do not. One has only to look at the data on student success to know that we are not making much progress with reaching poor children. There are many articles and books in the field that discuss the reasons why this is true, so I will not spend time here rehashing what we already know. Instead, I want to offer the following solutions based on the research and data available.

1. WE MUST PROVIDE POOR CHILDREN WITH THE VERY BEST TEACHERS AVAILABLE

I worked in a large city school district that had an unwritten rule, "If you mess up, your punishment will be that you will be transferred to a poor school." I wonder how many schools across the country adhere to that same rule. We need to reverse that thinking. Make it a reward to work with children from diverse backgrounds by providing teachers with the structures they need to be successful. Namely, give teachers outstanding training on working with diverse learners; provide them with facilities, technology, and materials that rival the best schools; and provide a support system for those days when things do not go well. Think of a building with scaffolding adequate to withstand anything—even strong winds. We must give these teachers the scaffolding to be successful.

2. WE MUST PROVIDE A HIGH-QUALITY AND CHALLENGING CURRICULUM FOR EVERY STUDENT

Educators made an assumption in the last decade that if they just made kids feel good about themselves and the teacher, all would be well. They would achieve at a high level regardless of race, creed, ethnicity, and poverty level. The way to get to that point, many educators believed, was to "water down" the curriculum in order to provide more opportunities for success. While it is important that students feel good about the classroom, the subject, and the teacher, there is nothing about watering down the material that makes anyone feel better about themselves; just the opposite.

3. WE MUST UNDERSTAND THE CULTURE OF OUR STUDENTS: TACOS ON TUESDAY IS NOT CULTURAL LITERACY

Children from poverty often enter public schools with children from middle-class and affluent backgrounds who have had enriched experiences to prepare them for the classroom and learning. In other words, for many students the entrance to public schools is not a door but a gap. It is not that these students can't learn or won't learn; they often have not had the opportunities to learn. I am not just talking about the names of colors, their ABCs, and counting. I am talking also about setting goals, knowing what to do when things are not working, and understanding how to get along in a middle-class atmosphere. Public education is built around middle-class values, attitudes, and rules. Until this country begins to examine and structure early childhood programs so that every child in America has the opportunity to have rich experiences in day care, the gap will always begin at this early stage.

Ruby Payne (1996) wrote a stirring article for the *Instructional Leader* in which she discussed the hidden rules of cultures. The hidden rules "are the unspoken clueing systems that individuals use to indicate membership in a group." If we are ever to reach every student, if we are ever to have a 100% success rate, we must heighten our awareness of the cultural differences in the classroom and how they affect learning and behavior. Payne (1996) says,

> One of the most important patterns is the following: In middle class, work and achievement tend to be the driving forces in decision-making. In wealthy, the driving forces are the political, social, and financial connections. In generational poverty, the driving forces are survival, entertainment and relationships.

She uses the example of a student whose Halloween costume costs $30 but whose book bill is not paid. She says, "Relationships and entertainment are more important than achievement" (Payne, 1996). We cannot bridge the gap between students until we understand what made the gap.

To provide a bridge for students, there are some factors that must be present; we must get away from isolation practices. I have been in more than a few classrooms where minority students or students whose primary language is different are seated at the back of the room or in isolation from the rest of the classroom. Move their desks to the front of the room and in proximity to the other students. They need the interaction and the attention.

Second, we must build relationships. Payne (1996) says,

> For students from generational poverty to learn, a significant relationship must be present. When individuals who made it out of poverty were interviewed, virtually all cite an individual who made a significant difference for them. Not only must the relationship be present, but also the academic tasks need to be referenced in terms of relationships.

As I stated in Chapter 1, we can raise the IQ level of students by as much as 20 points just by the climate we create.

Third, we must teach students the social skills they will need to be successful in the world they will enter. Part of the hidden rules is that different cultures are taught to react differently in stress situations. Children from generational poverty are taught to laugh in the face of adversity so that they do not show fear. Payne (1996) explains that a student who laughs when disciplined, however, will face further discipline. Schools tend to be built around middle-class standards that require a change in behavior and contriteness after discipline. I do not advocate that we accept laughter after discipline as okay, but I do believe that we need to educate students about what is the expected behavior. This is an important lesson if these students are to be successful in a world that is built around middle-class rules. As Payne (1996) says, "The recommended approach is simply to teach the student that he needs a set of rules that bring success in school and work and a set that brings success outside of school."

Fourth, we must desegregate state and national norm tests to be sure that no individual group is being overlooked academically. Often, when scores are high for a group, the low scores of a single, small group can be masked. We must not be content with scores until all groups are successful.

Fifth, where the cognitive structures are not in place, we must take the time to provide them. I have already discussed the importance of building brain connections (see Chapter 3). We cannot assume that any student already has the cognitive structure in place to connect the new learning. We must find out if the structure is there and, if not, we must provide it.

No longer can we be resigned to saying that some students just won't be successful. Whose child are we willing to sacrifice? Mine? Yours? *Breaking Ranks* (NASSP, 1996) says,

> Teachers must prepare themselves to take on the challenge of lifting the learning levels of students whose failures have been lamented but accepted. Right now, it is a given that some students will learn and some will not. High schools tend to let everyone squeeze by—even most of those who are actually learning very little of an academic nature—as if moving on a conveyor belt. But the reality of American education is that some students are embarked upon a trip to nowhere.

4. WE MUST FIND WAYS TO BUILD SELF-EFFICACY

Not all students come to us with the scaffolding in place to be successful. They may not have the language acquisition skills to be able to put factual information into long-term memory. (The semantic memory system relies on words—if I do not know and understand the words, I will either not store the information or will store it in such a way that I cannot retrieve it.) They may not know the hidden rules of the middle class upon which public schools operate. They may not know how to set goals or what to do when a goal is not working out. Students who do not know how to plan and adjust will acquiesce at the first sign of trouble. That is why we get students who begin a project or work, but do not finish.

We must directly teach students the skills necessary to be successful. Self-efficacy is the belief that I can do something because I have encountered success in the past. Self-efficacy believes that I have the necessary information, resources, and support to be successful. When we do not give students our instructional expectations up front, when we test on items that were not taught or that were not taught well, or when we do not directly teach the skills necessary to carry out the assignment, we limit self-efficacy in our classrooms. I call it the "gotchas." Provide students with the goals for the learning, lead them to set personal goals for their own learning, give them a matrix that shows them what they have to do to be successful, and test what you teach. It is a simple formula for success that is proven.

5. WE MUST BE RABID ABOUT ELIMINATING BIAS

In my book *What Every Teacher Should Know About Diverse Learners* (Tileston, 2004a), I talk about the types of bias from Gibbs (1994). For the purposes of this book, I will provide the list of categories and a brief explanation of each. Tileston (2004a) defines each as follows:

- Linguistic Bias—Linguistic bias includes any language that is dehumanizing or denies the existence of a certain group. This includes laughing at students' names or teaching history without acknowledging the contributions of minorities.

- Stereotyping—Stereotyping is a form of bias that occurs when we assume that a given set of criteria apply to all members of a group. This includes showing minorities in supporting roles rather than leadership roles, females with limits on what professions they can enter, and disabled students as helpless. Look at books, materials, and visuals used in the classroom to remove this bias.

- Exclusion—Exclusion is the lack of representation from a group. It can also be the removal of a group from the larger group based on race, ethnicity, religion, or gender. At one time, in this country, students who learned in a different modality from the teaching or who came to school without the prerequisite skills were placed in Title I or special education programs incorrectly.

- Unreality—Unreality is the misinformation about a group, event, or contribution. We do this when we lower our expectations for students based on preconceived ideas, such as how their siblings did in our classrooms.

- Selectivity—Selectivity is the single interpretation of an issue, situation, or condition. We do this when we fail to understand the cultural backgrounds of our students and assume that all students will come to us with middle-class values and understandings.

- Isolation—Isolation is the separating of groups. Isolation takes place when grouping centers around all-male or all-female groups or groups based on ethnicity.

6. WE MUST WORK WITH COMMUNITY LEADERS TO PROVIDE SUPPORT FOR THESE STUDENTS

Poverty is not just lack of wealth; it is lack of services as well. Tileston (2004a) says,

> The solutions are not confined to the schools, but must be a part of a unified effort on the part of national, state, and local entities that work hand in hand with parents and the school. In order for poor students to

be able to compete on a level playing field, they must have the quality health, nutrition, and other resources that are a part of the package of essentials provided to children who do not come from poverty.

Wang and Kovach (1996) agree: "Narrowly conceived plans and commitment that focus only on schools will not solve the growing problems that must be addressed to ensure success of the many children and youth who have not fared will under the current system of service delivery."

Payne (2001) describes wealth as the amount of available resources. Resources include more than money. A strong support system, role models, the ability to work within the middle-class framework, being physically and mentally healthy, and having money to purchase both goods and services make up the differences between wealth and poverty. Just because parents are poor does not mean that they do not care. Often they do not have the skills or the ability to help their children to be successful. All parents can be encouraging and can value education.

We need to be strong advocates in the communities in which we teach for parent support. Begin with the leaders of the community—even poor communities have leaders. Set up parent groups to help you achieve the goals of your classroom and your school. One of my schools has a committee called the VIP (Very Important Parents) Committee, which heads up school open house, parent committees, school functions, and so forth. They have taken some of the work off of teachers and have been able to get parents to school when the best efforts of the school personnel have failed.

Help students find and use needed medical and social services. Be an advocate for helping organizations join hands to provide much needed services for these students.

7. WE MUST CHANGE OUR WAY OF THINKING

There was a time in this country when education assumed that only a few would be successful. This type of thinking was based on the bell curve model. Some would be successful, some would fail, and the majority would fall somewhere in the middle. Later, we came to understand that more children would be successful if given more time, more resources, and so forth. The saying of the time was "All kids can learn." Today, we know not only that kids can learn but also that they *must* learn. We cannot afford a generation that does not read, cannot do basic math, and cannot articulate their ideas to others.

We will not change the dynamics of poverty until we do something about education. This means that we must begin now to provide a quality preschool program for the poor and we must utilize that time to help provide the scaffolding needed to be successful in school from the beginning. While that scaffolding is a knowledge of letter sounds, a familiarity with numbers, and a love for books, that is only part of the underpinning. We must teach children how to plan, how to use self-talk, and what to do when plans are not going well. We must instruct them in the hidden rules upon which school and work depend.

CONCLUSION

When efforts are consciously made to bridge the gap between all learners, test data on students will be analyzed from a variety of perspectives. The data will be massaged for trends, highs, lows, and each represented group. Teachers and staff will stay abreast of the latest research on how students learn through staff development and education literature. In addition, the teacher will use direct teaching techniques to help provide cognitive structures where none exists. Perhaps most important, the climate in the classroom will be, at all times, a supportive and nurturing one where building relationships is a priority and where there will be no hidden agendas.

Figure 7.1 shows the indicators that will be present when all students are successful.

Figure 7.1   Indicators That the Gap Between All Learners Has Been Bridged

Assessment Tool	Indicators of Success
Test data	Will be analyzed for trends, highs, lows, and each represented group
Observations	Relationships will be a priority in the classroom
Student products	Indicate that instruction has been designed to solicit, incorporate, and build upon the knowledge, experiences, and perspectives of all students
Staff training	Indicates that teachers stay abreast of latest trends and methodologies for all student groups

8

Evaluating Learning Through a Variety of Authentic Assessments

Assessment is a fact of life, whether we like it or not. We are all being assessed daily according to the decisions we make and the way in which we carry out those decisions. Our students are being held accountable to the public for declarative and procedural information through myriad tests designed to show competency and used at the state and national level for comparison of schools (Tileston, 2004e).

Assessment begins with effective planning on the part of the teacher and the students. As teachers, we must ask ourselves what it is that we want students to know and be able to do as a result of the learning. Only then can we effectively plan our lessons. Lessons should begin with the end in mind. What is important for students to know and understand? Grant Wiggins and Jay McTighe (1998) describe a lesson design that looks at performance first. Before teachers build the lesson, they ask these critical questions:

- What enabling knowledge (facts, concepts, and principles) and skills (procedures) will students need to perform effectively to achieve desired results?
- What activities will equip students with the needed knowledge and skills?
- What will need to be taught and coached, and how should it best be taught, in light of performance goals?

- What materials and resources are best suited to accomplish these goals?
- Is the overall design coherent and effective?

Assessment is built on declarative and procedural objectives written and provided to students prior to the lessons.

DECLARATIVE INFORMATION

Declarative objectives are based on what students will know as a result of the teaching and learning process. Declarative objectives are factual in nature and are taught with different tools than procedural objectives. Declarative objectives are stored in a different part of the brain than procedural objectives. So it stands to reason that successful implementation and assessment must begin with the type of objectives being employed. Declarative objectives for a lesson on nouns and pronouns might look something like this:

Declarative Objectives: Students will know the following:

- The definition of a noun
- The definition of a pronoun
- The rules for the use of a noun
- The rules for the use of a pronoun

For a lesson on shapes, the declarative goals might look like this:

Students will know the following facts:

- The vocabulary words associated with shapes (i.e., square, rectangle, circle, cone, triangle)
- The attributes of various shapes
- Why the study of shapes is important

Notice that all of the objectives are based on the students acquiring knowledge. They are not doing anything with the information at this point; they are gathering the facts that they will need to use the knowledge. Definitions, rules, and facts make up declarative objectives.

Assessing Declarative Knowledge

Most testing of declarative information is through what Stiggens (1994) calls *forced-choice assessment*. He defines forced-choice assessment as follows: "The respondent is asked a series of questions, each of which is accompanied by a range of alternative responses. The respondent's task is to select either the correct or the best answer from among the options. The index of achievement is the number or proportion of questions answered correctly."

Examples of forced-choice assessment include multiple-choice, matching, true-false, multiple-response, and fill-in-the-blank tests. My book *What Every Teacher Should Know About Student Assessment* (Tileston, 2004e) discusses these test types and provides an example for each.

We also assess declarative knowledge through questioning and other forms of dialogue with students or through students interacting with each other using techniques such as cooperative learning.

PROCEDURAL KNOWLEDGE

Next, students need to know what they will do with these definitions, rules, and facts. These are the procedural objectives for the lesson. Procedural objectives, as the name implies, require the learner to employ a process to the learning. Procedural objectives for our lesson on nouns and pronouns might look like this:

Procedural Objectives: Students will be able to do the following:

- Distinguish between a noun and a pronoun
- Use the appropriate pronoun for the given noun
- Use capitalization correctly
- Write sentences using correct pronouns from a given prompt
- Write a paragraph using nouns and pronouns appropriately
- Justify their use of a pronoun from a given prompt
- Explain in their own words the difference between a noun and a pronoun

For our lesson on shapes, the procedural objectives might look like this:

Students will be able to do the following processes:

- Identify the various shapes from drawings
- Draw the shapes themselves
- Identify shapes from their surroundings; for example, on windows, doors, and furniture

Procedural objectives take the knowledge of the declarative objectives to a more complex level, one at which the student demonstrates that he or she can use the information. When planning, the teacher asks, "What activities do I need to include in the lessons to determine that my students can use the information provided through the declarative objectives?"

Assessing Procedural Knowledge

In addition to the activities designed by the teacher to provide opportunities to use the declarative information, the following methods are often used to assess procedural knowledge.

Figure 8.1   Example of an Essay Question That Requires Procedural Knowledge

Since the start of the school year, your class has been studying the principles and procedures used in chemical analysis. One of your friends has missed several weeks of class because of illness and is worried about a major exam in chemistry that will be given in two weeks. This friend asks you to explain everything that she will need to know for the exam.

Write an essay in which you explain the most important ideas and principles that your friend should understand. In your essay, you should include general concepts and specific facts you know about chemistry, and especially what you know about chemical analysis or identifying unknown substances. You should also explain how the teacher's demonstration illustrates important principles of chemistry. Be sure to show the relationships among the ideas, facts, and procedures you know.

Essays

Tileston (2004e) says, "The strength of essay-type assessments is in the stem for the essay itself. What do you want to know? Do you want to know if students understand the facts or do you want to know if they can use reasoning, problem-solving techniques, or decision-making?" An example of an essay question that requires students to use higher-level thinking comes from the Web site for the Center for Research on Evaluation, Standards, and Student Testing (CRESST, www.cresst.org; see Figure 8.1).

Short Written Responses. Tests that ask for short written responses are really a form of the essay, but are limited to very specific information. These questions might only address declarative information, but they can address procedural as well. The advantage to these types of tests is that, when carefully constructed, the questions test higher-level thinking. For example, for a short written response that tests only declarative information, elementary or middle school students might be asked to list the sequence of events in the chapter titled "Finders Keepers" from *Henry Huggins*, by Beverly Cleary. A procedural question might ask, In the story, the main character finds a dog that he wants to keep for his own. When the rightful owner shows up, our main character must make a decision. Make a list of possible solutions for the problem. Be sure to include at least three solutions that are your own ideas. Create a list of four criteria for making the decision about which of your options to use. Based on your criteria, which option will you chose? Defend your answer.

Oral Reports

Oral reports are an auditory form of the essay and may include both declarative and procedural information.

Performance Tasks

Quality performance tasks can be an excellent way of assessing students' learning. However, performance tasks are often rote and low level. For this type of measurement to be useful, the task should reach higher levels of thinking and should require students to truly understand the topics studied.

All performance tasks, whether they are homework or independent projects, should include a matrix or rubric by the teacher so that students know exactly what is meant by a quality product. Whenever I think about quality products, I am reminded of an experience that I had with my own son. In the school that we restructured, we decided as a faculty that we would accept only quality work. We took to heart Deming's (1986) words, "Do it right the first time and every time," and we made believers of our students. In the past, our gifted students had not been truly challenged. They could usually slop something together and turn it in for an "A" because it was still better than what the other students were turning in. But this was a new year and our expectations were higher for those "other kids." Our students who had traditionally not done well in school were suddenly turning in quality work, and whenever you raise the floor, you have to raise the ceiling. So, for the first time, gifted students were truly being challenged to do work at a higher level.

One afternoon I came home from work to find my own son, who was in the gifted program, working diligently on a project for English class. He was studying British literature and was creating a shield fashioned after the shields used in England to depict information about the family that bore them. Each section of the shield was to depict different characteristics of his beliefs and heritage. I had a parent meeting to go to, so I left him working in the living room. I wasn't much concerned about the state of the living room with his materials strewn everywhere, because I knew he would be finished by the time I returned. His group of friends adhered to the 15-minute rule on homework: If it were going to take more than 15 minutes, they would get on the phone and divide up the work. They were into cooperative learning long before we added it to the curriculum.

Imagine my surprise when I returned about 9:30 to find that he was still busy at the project. I took one look at the living room and said, "Kevin, just push all this stuff to the side, we'll clean it up tomorrow. I want to go to bed." He frowned. "I can't, I'm not finished with my shield. There is one part that I can't do. I know what I want to say, but I can't draw it. It's the part about my political view. If I tell you what I want to say will you draw it for me?" Now, I have a limited amount of artistic ability—I mainly draw only for family and friends—so on most nights I would not have minded the task. However, I had been up since 6:00 that morning, I had worked all day, and I had met with parents that night. So, I said, "Just cut something out of a magazine and paste it on; I want to go to bed." He replied, "You don't understand. It's a matter of quality!" We had saved one gifted child.

Teacher Observation

We have focused so much on student's feeling good about themselves that we have often been too positive or general in our praise. For teacher feedback to be effective, it must be specific, sincere, and both diagnostic and prescriptive. Let me show you what I mean. Saying "good job" to a student is not feedback. Feedback might sound something like this: "Jim, you have done a great job at writing your beginning goal for the learning. This has a personal interest for you. Now, think about why we might spend time at school on this topic? Why would it be important for people to know in life? How might you use this information in other situations? How will this help you to be a better citizen? Family member?"

In most instances, declarative objectives are taught before the procedural objectives. The declarative objectives provide the scaffolding for the procedural. These goals should be provided to students visually. For older students, put them up in the room and refer to them often. Goal setting is an important part of the teaching-learning process. Refer to them frequently so that students can measure their own learning. For young students, put them up using visual symbols. Also, send them home to parents so that you have a baseline of support for what you are trying to accomplish with the class. Ask students to write personal goals for the learning. In Chapter 1, we discussed why the learning must have personal meaning to our students. Personal meaning is a brain-friendly way to tap into the self-system of the brain.

Authentic assessment looks at both declarative and procedural objectives.

RUBRICS AND MATRICES

The next step in authentic assessment is for the teacher to provide to the students the criteria for success. This might be in the form of a rubric, a matrix, or written steps. Except with very young children, this information should be written and it should be in the hands of every student. The rubric alone is a form of self-assessment for the students, since they should be given opportunities to refer to it often to determine how well they are learning. For the lesson on nouns and pronouns, the rubric might look like Figure 8.2.

Note that in the rubric provided in Figure 8.2, items numbered 1 and 2 relate to the declarative information while the rest of the items relate to the processes employed using the declarative information. So often, assessment is limited to declarative objectives. By deliberately writing the objectives as both declarative and procedural, we are more likely to assess both.

Anything for which we are taking a grade or making an assessment should have criteria that are given to the students upfront, before the assignment— even homework. This takes the "gotcha" out of assessment. Figure 8.3 is an example of a matrix for mathematics homework, which was originally published in my book *What Every Teacher Should Know About Student Assessment* (Tileston, 2004e).

CONCLUSION

Good assessment reflects both declarative and procedural information. To do all this, schools must ask some hard questions about the assessment. Does the assessment provide adequate information about the degree of learning? What is the appropriate vehicle for the assessment? Has adequate time been allowed to ensure that assessment of long-term memory is taking place, not just

Figure 8.2   Matrix for Nouns and Pronouns

Great Job	*You Are On Your Way*	*Not There Yet*
1. The student understands the vocabulary words and can state them in his or her own words.	1. The student can recite the vocabulary words and definitions but has difficulty putting them into his or her own words or defending the definitions.	1. The student has merely memorized the vocabulary and definitions. There is little if any understanding or ownership to them.
2. The student understands the rules and attributes that identify a noun and a pronoun and can use those rules to create and use his or her own nouns and pronouns for writing.	2. The student knows the rules and attributes of both the noun and pronoun but still struggles at times to remember some of the rules.	2. The student cannot appropriately use the rules for the noun and pronoun consistently
3. The student demonstrates understanding of the mechanics of using a noun or pronoun correctly by supplying the correct form in given prompts. The student can defend in his or her words the rules that are employed.	3. The student demonstrates understanding of the mechanics of using nouns and pronouns most of the time with some prompting but may not be able to defend his or her choices consistently.	3. The student demonstrates a surface knowledge of the use of nouns and pronouns, but can only use them correctly with prompting by the teacher.

memorization for the short term? What is important to measure? Do we need to measure the process, the product, or both? More important, does the assessment truly reflect the learning? Is it more important that students are able to name the date of the Yalta Agreement or that they know the process to find that date, should they need it?

Assessment should be an active demonstration of students' understanding and their ability to apply this understanding. Marlowe and Page (1998) tell us,

> To create assessment instruments that do more than merely tap a student's recall or recognition skills, we must reframe assessment so that
>
> - It is, as much as possible, a continuous process that is part of instruction and not separate from it.
> - Connects directly to learning and is introduced before or simultaneously with material
> - It requires students to do more than simply remember (e.g., requires students to develop mathematical formulas, produce

Figure 8.3 Matrix for Homework

Criteria	Attributes
All problems worked	• Steps followed correctly • All work shown • Work is checked
Understanding of mathematics is evident	• Explains work thoroughly • Is able to justify answers • Is able to explain the process to others
Work is turned in at a timely interval	• Work is on time • Work is complete
Work is legible	• Work is neat and legible • Work can be easily seen and understood

exhibitions, write essays, create a sculpture, write poetry, create a musical score, develop and participate in debates, or create and conduct experiments).

• Student questions, at least in part, drive the process.

We need to know that students can construct meaning from the learning. In my book *What Every Teacher Should Know About Student Assessment* (Tileston, 2004e), I paraphrase Wiggins and McTighe (1998), who say that when students truly understand, they can:

• explain in their own words,
• interpret by reading between the lines to give additional and plausible information,
• apply by transferring information from one format or situation to another,
• see in perspective by justifying a position as a point of view,
• demonstrate empathy for others' points of view,
• reveal self-knowledge by identifying their own ideas, feelings, strengths, and weaknesses.

There is no way that we can teach students everything they need to know in order to be successful. First of all, we don't know what will be necessary for them to know in their lifetimes to be successful. We must give them tools to formulate understanding, structures for problem solving, and research retrieval skills, and then we must assess to see if they can use these tools. We do this by giving them assessment exercises that employ those processes. Independent projects, experiments, and complex problem solving are some of the ways this can be accomplished.

We discussed in Chapter 5 the importance of setting high expectations for student products. The teacher needs to set the standard high and give specific parameters for the expected project. While it is important to give students choices, it is equally important to set parameters to ensure that the final product reflects quality. Instead of saying to students that we want a research project on the brain and learning, we might say instead that we want a research project on the brain and learning that includes, at a minimum, the work of Jensen and Sousa. We might also let them choose the format of the finished product. For example, the finished product might be written as a monograph on the need for changes in education, presented in a multimedia format using PowerPoint, or dramatized as a student forum. Students have choices, but the teacher sets the parameters for the level of quality. The highest level a product can attain is that of providing usefulness beyond the person who created it.

Ellis and Fouts (1997) say, "In a more perfect educational world, it would be impossible to separate assessment procedures from curriculum content." If assessment is authentic, it should be closely aligned to the day-to-day experiences of the curriculum.

Figure 8.4 shows indicators that will be present when authentic assessment is practiced.

Figure 8.4   Indicators That a Variety of Assessments That Authentically Evaluate the Learner Are Used

Assessment Tool	Indicators of Success
Student products	Demonstrate understanding by being able to use the learning in different contexts
Student products	Indicate student use of a variety of inquiry skills to solve problems, create products, and access information
Student assessments	Indicate a wide range, reflect the learning, and follow the rubric
Student assessments	Indicate learning beyond state and national standards

9

In-Depth Understanding That Leads to Real-World Practices

Since our brain is designed to learn for survival, it is very good at learning that which it perceives to be useful, practical and real.

—Eric Jensen, *Completing the Puzzle* (1997)

There is no way that we can teach students everything that they will need to know in life. When I was in school, many of the diseases and problems that we face today had not even been envisioned. My teachers could not teach me about diseases such as AIDS or even how to vote on the issues involved. What they could do was provide me with the in-depth skills needed to make informed decisions. That is not to say that we should not teach students factual information; declarative information is critical to the basics of education. What I am saying is that students need to know how they learned the information and how to apply the processes of learning so that they can transfer those processes to real-world issues throughout their lives. In Chapter 3, a model for a KNLH chart is provided. The H in the chart stands for "How did I learn." Students need to realize which processes were utilized to learn material. Information does not become a part of long-term memory until we believe that we know it.

Jensen (1997) lists four stages of understanding—starter knowledge, relational knowledge, globalized knowledge, and expert knowledge. Using Jensen's four stages as a basis, let's examine each and the processes that lead to students becoming experts in the learning.

STAGE ONE: STARTER KNOWLEDGE

The starter knowledge stage of learning is sometimes referred to as surface knowledge. Students are memorizing facts that may or may not have any specific meaning to them. For example, students may be learning the components of the periodic table in science, the definitions of shapes in mathematics, the reasons for World War II in history, or the sequence of events in a story. This type of information is usually assessed by paper-and-pencil tests where students merely prove that they have memorized the information. The real-world application is low at best, and more often students are not even aware of how they learned the information or of the application to the real world.

STAGE TWO: RELATIONAL KNOWLEDGE

In the relational knowledge stage of the learning, students are making connections across disciplines and time. When they study the reasons for World War II, they are looking for patterns that cause conflicts and analyzing current world situations for similarities. Instead of just learning the names and dimensions of shapes, they are finding those shapes all around them. They no longer look at a story for its parts, but for patterns that can be applied to other situations. Dr. Seuss's *Sneeches* is not just a funny story about fuzzy green animals with stars in the middle of their stomachs, but comments on a pattern of behavior (prejudice, exclusivity) that occurs in life. The conflicts in *Hamlet* are a picture of similar conflicts that occur throughout history.

Students have to do something with the learning at this level. That might include integrating information, mind mapping the information, or looking for patterns. It might include physically finding similarities, such as a tour of the school to find shapes or an examination of wheelchair ramps to determine slope. Wiggins and McTighe (1998) say that students at this stage can explain the information.

STAGE THREE: GLOBALIZED KNOWLEDGE

Students who participate in globalized knowledge understand the impact of the knowledge beyond their immediate world. They understand the impact to their community, country, world, and planet. At this point, the learning takes on a more in-depth, personal meaning as students examine their own belief systems and how they feel about the issues involved. This type of learning is more likely to stay with the student throughout life—not just for the test on Friday. They see things from other points of view and they have a better understanding of

Figure 9.1   What?, So What?, and Now What?

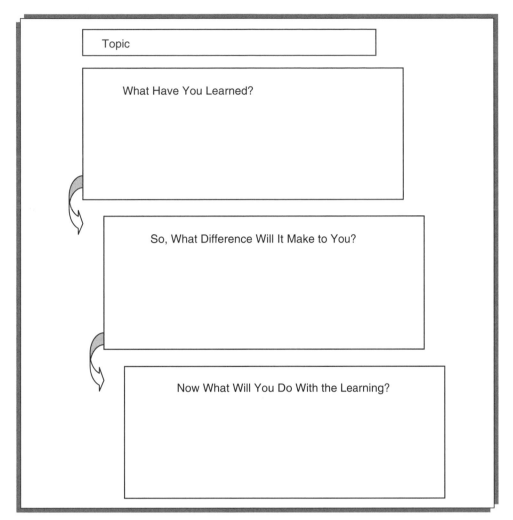

the value of the information and processes that they have acquired. In the example in Figure 9.1, students can fully answer the question, "Now what?"

"What?, So What?, and Now What?" is a reflection exercise that helps students think about the learning and its usefulness to them personally and beyond. The "What?" stands for "What have you learned?" Students list facts and ideas that have surfaced as a result of the learning. The "So What?" stands for "So, what difference will it make to you?" Students write, in their own words, the personal application of the learning to their lives. The "Now What?" stands for "Now what will you do with the learning?" At this stage, students look beyond the present to how the information might be used in the future and beyond themselves. They must be able to make connections to complete this part of the exercise. Reflection is an important part of any lesson, because until students believe that they have learned, the learning will not be real to them.

Figure 9.2   Prediction Tree

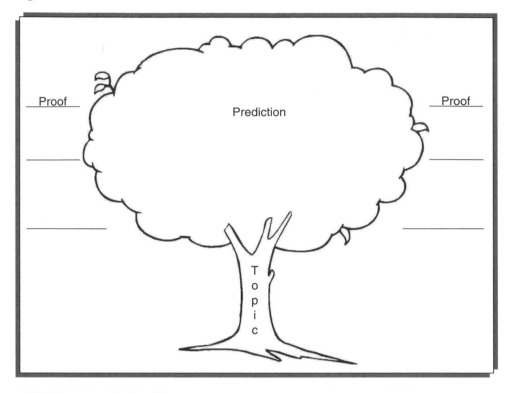

Wiggins and McTighe (1998) say that students at this stage can see perspectives.

STAGE FOUR: EXPERT KNOWLEDGE

Students at the expert knowledge stage are insightful and can apply the information in a variety of contexts. They employ all six of the facets of understanding provided by Wiggins and McTighe (1998). They can do the following:

1. Explain what they know in their own words. Students not only explain in their own words, but, as this ability is developed, they can justify their interpretations. They will have the ability to decide what is the underlying problem or central fact. They will also be able to predict, based on fact. Figure 9.2 is a graphic organizer that I use to teach students to be able to make good predictions. In this figure, students are given basic facts and information and then asked to make a prediction about what will happen next. Notice that their predictions must be based on facts and they have to be able to justify the facts.

2. Interpret information and processes, including hidden meanings. At a higher level, these students can "read between the lines and offer plausible

accounts of the many possible purposes and meanings of any text (i.e., book, situation or human behavior)" (Wiggins & McTighe, 1998).

3. Apply information in real-world contexts. The student can project the information into a variety of contexts other than the classroom.

4. See their own perspective and the perspective of others. This includes critiquing information for its worth. Wiggins and McTighe (1998) say that the student with expert knowledge can also do the following:

- Know the limits as well as the power of an idea
- See through argument or language that is biased, partisan, or ideological
- See and explain the importance or worth of an idea

5. Demonstrate empathy for the ideas and assumptions of others. The learner truly understands the motivations and views of others even when the learner does not agree with those ideas.

6. Understand themselves in terms of prejudices, understandings, and limitations. The learner participates in thinking about the learning and self-assessing accurately. An expert learner will have the ability to accept feedback and put it to use.

CONCLUSION

In a classroom where real-world application to the learning is actually applied, there will be evidence in the lesson that the knowledge has been connected to authentic situations that occur outside the classroom as well as within. Moreover, students will be given opportunities to reflect on the learning as evidenced by journals and written guided reflections. Depth of understanding will be evident through journals, products, and written materials, and a part of assessment will be the student's ability to tie the learning to real-world situations.

Figure 9.3 shows the indicators that will be present when real-world application is applied to the learning.

Figure 9.3   Indicators That Instruction Promotes Real-World Application of the Learning

Assessment Tools	Indicators of Success
Lesson plans	Indicate that the knowledge has been applied to authentic situations that occur outside the classroom as well as within
Journals and student products	Indicate depth of understanding and opportunities for reflection
Assessments	Indicate students' understanding of real-world application

Seamless Integration of Technology for High-Quality Instruction

S tudents enter our school hallways each day fresh from a digital world that not only allows them to communicate throughout the world, but also gives them the ability to solve problems, do research, and perform at levels never before available in the history of man. Those same students often go to classrooms where the primary learning tools are lecture, note taking, and rote learning. No wonder they drop out mentally.

At the Graves County Schools in Kentucky, students receive local credits for helping teachers create innovative and high-tech lessons for the classroom. The idea was conceived when students complained that lessons were often low level and out of touch with the multimedia world from which these students come. Ten teachers volunteered for the first year of the program, which includes high school students assigned to them to help facilitate the learning through technology. They have not stopped with the lessons, but have also pursued other communications as well—for example, teacher Web sites to keep parents and students informed.

In the preceding chapters, nine best practices were discussed. All of these practices can be greatly enhanced by the use of good technology. As a matter of fact, technology is the vehicle that can help shift classrooms to best practices.

In Chapter 1, climate and its powerful effect on student learning were discussed. Through the use of technology, teachers will more effectively be able to monitor and provide anytime, anywhere assistance to students. Through

Internet and Intranet resources, students will be able to get assignments, additional help, and clarifications online. Students who are absent or unable to attend classes can learn online. Students will have more choices as a whole world of learning opportunities becomes available. Telementoring will be the wave of the future as students are linked to adults with like interests and abilities through e-mail. Ann Foster (1999) quotes a 1995 impact study of Big Brothers/Big Sisters of America that shows, "Young people with mentors are 46 percent less likely to begin using illegal drugs, 27 percent less likely to begin using alcohol, 53 percent less likely to skip school, 37 percent less likely to skip a class, and 33 percent less likely to hit someone." A mentor who can be accessed anytime, anywhere is a step forward from the mentoring programs of the past that took place only on certain days of the week and at specified times.

Tileston (2004d) lists the following reasons why technology is brain friendly:

- Technology is not limited by the classroom walls.
- Technology does not know or care what the student's socioeconomic status may be and thus helps level the playing field for these students.
- Technology provides an equal opportunity for everyone to learn.
- Technology is more in tune with the way our students today learn.
- Technology is so much a part of the real world that to limit its use in the classroom is to limit our students' ability to compete in the world. In "The Net Generation and the School" (1998), Don Tapscott says this "Net Generation" watches much less television than did its parents. Tapscott cites a 1997 survey by Teenage Research Unlimited, in which 80% of the teenagers polled said it is "in" to be online—right up there with dating and partying.

In Chapter 2, the need to address the various learning styles of students was outlined. Much software is available to the classroom today that incorporates visual, verbal, and kinesthetic learning. Software tools allow the teacher who is unfamiliar with visual models to create them easily and effortlessly just by plugging in his or her teaching outline. Students who need visuals to learn, students who are dyslexic and need graphic representations, will be able to view the learning in a format that is comfortable and meaningful to them. Lessons can be more interesting with the addition of multimedia formats that more closely mirror the world from which our students come. Just adding PowerPoint presentations to low-technology tools, such as chalkboard and overheads, would add a new dimension to teaching and learning.

In Chapter 3, I discussed the need to help students make connections from prior learning to the new learning. Through technology, students will be able to view the learning as well as hear it. They will also have the opportunity individually to review past information. Through the use of animation and visuals, teachers will be able to give the learning relevance to a degree not possible in the past. Talking about polar bears to children who live in southern regions has much less relevance than taking them through virtual classrooms to a zoo or a region where they can see real polar bears.

Technology opens up a whole new world of learning to those students who need visual representations. I recently volunteered to read to a group of first graders in a school near me. When the teacher brought the children to the library for the lesson, she sat one child off to the side by himself. She whispered to me that he would probably not sit quietly for the lesson and that she was placing him so that she could easily remove him from the room if necessary. Instead of just reading the book to the children, as we so often do, I read the book as I showed selected pictures from the story using PowerPoint software and an LCD projection device that showed the pictures from my computer on a television monitor. Not only did the young man in question sit quietly for the story, but when I had finished, he yelled, "Do it again!" This was a visual child in an auditory world and he had already become a discipline problem in first grade because he was being forced to learn in a modality not comfortable for him.

At a Texas Rangers baseball game, I was amazed at the powerful teaching tools that were used on the huge multimedia screen in the park. Points came across easily and in short periods of time with the video clips, animated words, and pictures that flashed often across the screen. A long ball to right field might bring an animated "Wow!" on the screen. The productivity tools are available now to make dynamic, exciting presentations in the classroom. An emotional "Wow!" every once in a while would be good for us all.

In Chapter 4, the need to help students put the information into long-term memory rather than just memorizing for a test was addressed. The sensory devices that are a part of technology will allow teachers to enrich their lessons for the classroom. Research projects have greater relevance when students encounter information and concepts through virtual classrooms, distance learning, the Internet, and worldwide e-mail. Student projects take on a new dimension with technology as their guide. Semantic memory will be enhanced by technology because relevance or meaning will be more evident as students are able to apply information to authentic situations and problems. Student projects can be created virtually so that immediate relevance is seen rather than having to wait until a time in the future when students have jobs that deal with real problems.

Teachers can enhance episodic memory by using technology to create props or tools that trigger recall. A prop as simple as a red tennis shoe created by technology to prompt students to remember the rules for using verbs is a simple example of how episodic memory can be enhanced through technology.

In Chapter 5, the importance of teaching to higher-level thinking in the classroom was reported. Technology assists with this by providing a rich environment for research. The possibilities are limitless. By using good productivity tools, the quality of products that students can produce is enhanced. Written reports take on a new dimension when the student is able to add animation and other visuals in a PowerPoint or similar presentation. An added bonus is that, with technology, students can work on their project anytime, anywhere rather than having to rely on the office hours of libraries or museums. A group of high school students used technology to study the force of motion on roller coasters by setting up their rides and then measuring the G-forces. This type of experiment would not be possible without technology, since human subjects could experience whiplash or worse while the project was in its experimental stages.

In Chapter 6, the need for collaboration was emphasized. Technology opens all the windows and doors to make this possible. Parents may not be able to come to the school, but the school can come to them through e-mail, the Internet, distance learning, and virtual classes. Schools can communicate better with all of the stakeholders through virtual opportunities. Student projects and studies will not be limited to the students in the classroom. Students can work with other students in the building and in other schools as well. Teachers can communicate with each other literally anytime, anywhere. Collaboration takes on a whole new meaning with technology.

The need to reach 100% of the students was revealed in Chapter 7. Technology is the tool that will lead the way to making education equitable for all students, regardless of their background. The computer does not see race, wealth, gender, or beliefs: It is a great equalizer. The hidden agendas of society are not a factor there. Schools that need and want to bridge the gap should be actively pursuing the resources to make high-level technology possible. Governments that tout high standards must come to realize that high standards require high-level tools. The future of education rests on two things: First, quality teachers who not only can teach in the traditional classroom but also in a nontraditional setting and who can inspire; second, technology that is of a high level and that mirrors the real world. These are the gateways to produce a quality product.

The authentic assessments in Chapter 8 take on a higher level of quality when we add productivity tools. Students will also be able to create electronic portfolios and logs that help track and showcase growth. An electronic portfolio is probably a better tool for university and job applications than the traditional test scores and grades. If completed properly, the portfolios show the multitalents of the individual rather than the single ability to take tests.

Nothing is more real-world than the experience of being in the place discussed, conversing with the people being studied, or watching practitioners use the skills being learned. Through video conferencing, virtual classrooms, distance learning, and the Internet, all of these things are possible today.

These are not ideas for the future—I do not consider myself to be a futurist. These are the possibilities of now. Education should be so exciting, so exacting, that students would literally run to get to it. Technology will help make this a reality.

CONCLUSION

Schools that place a priority on technology provide technology that is accessible to everyone, all day, not just in laboratory situations. Both instructional technology, which deals with creating an optimum teaching and learning environment, and educational technology, which deals with technology literacy, are a vital part of the curriculum. Emphasis is on using productivity tools, not expensive drill-and-practice software, and student products reflect the use of those tools.

At a minimum, these schools provide access to the Internet, Intranet, and e-mail for teachers and students. Students learn processes that reflect technology use at a high level. Some examples are PowerPoint presentations beginning in elementary school, e-mail for student collaboration at all levels, and Web authoring by the secondary level. School Internet resources allow parents to retrieve information about student assignments, progress, and curriculum anytime.

Classes will not be limited to a single space or to a single building, but will be opened up to the possibilities of distance learning. Through technology, students will be able to take classes never before possible. The lines between school and college will be blurred as students take college and career courses along with their basic skills classes for high school graduation.

Through technology, the classroom takes on another dimension as the world—rather than the bricks-and-mortar building—becomes the classroom. Resources never before possible, relevance and depth of study at a level never before achieved in a classroom, and the exchange of ideas with unlimited possibilities boggle the mind. Technology is not an end in itself; it can lead us toward the type of classroom of which we have all dreamed.

Figure 10.1 shows the indicators that will be present when technology is utilized at a quality level.

Figure 10.1 Indicators That Technology Is Used at a Quality Level

Assessment Tools	Indicators of Success
Observation	Technology tools will be accessible to everyone
Observation	Technology will be integrated into the classroom, not relegated to an isolated lab setting
Student products	Indicate an emphasis on productivity tools, not expensive drill-and-practice software
Technology tools	Indicate that students and teachers have access to the Internet, Intranet, and e-mail
Student products	Indicate learning processes that reflect technology use at a high level
Parent surveys	Indicate access to school Internet and Intranet services to retrieve information from student assignments, progress, and curriculum anytime
Field trips	Reflect virtual trips to places heretofore not accessible to the school
Class offerings	Indicate that they are not limited by a single space or a single building, but offer possibilities through the Internet, distance learning, and video conferencing
Student products	Will indicate that students have been taught the elements of information retrieval, including the ability to discern between primary and secondary resources, the difference between fact and opinion, and the ethics of using technology responsibly
Lessons	Indicate the use of technology to make them more dynamic, emotional, and relevant

11

Putting It
All Together

"All men dream": but not equally. Those who dream by night in the dusty recesses of their mind wake in the day to find that it was vanity: but the dreamers of the day are dangerous men, for they may act their dream with open eyes, to make it possible.

—T. E. Lawrence, *Seven Pillars of Wisdom* (1935)

The 10 teaching practices offered in this book are only a beginning—but an important beginning. They provide a framework for classroom instruction that is very different from the instruction of the past centuries. This is not change, but a whole new way of looking at the learning process. We have never had so much information available to us before on how the brain works. We also have never had so many challenges before us as we do in today's very diverse surroundings. The classroom teacher has taken on roles beyond teaching. I often tell teacher groups that if all there was to teaching was just knowing our subject matter and providing it to students, we would not have a teacher shortage. The truth is that teachers are leaving the teaching field because the demands are sometimes overwhelming and the rules seem to be constantly changing.

In an article for *Newsweek*, Anna Quindlen (2004) lamented the fact that the war on poverty is far from won; some might even say that we are worse off. "Recently released figures from the Census Bureau show that for the third year in a row the number of Americans living below the poverty line has increased." She is quick to point out that the poverty line at this time is set quite low—at $18,000 per year for a family of four. "When you adjust the level to reflect reality, you come closer to 35 percent of all Americans who are having a hard time providing the basics for their families, what the Community Service Society of New York calls 'The Unheard Third.'"

As you look for solutions to your school's problems and as you work to incorporate the ideas from this book, the following check list from *What Every Teacher Should Know About Diverse Learners* (Tileston, 2004a) may be of help to you.

The following checklist is offered as a guide for schools as they begin to look toward ways to not only narrow the achievement gap but to close it.

What will we do?

In our country and in our states

- ☐ Be cognizant of the attitudes and plans of lawmakers and political candidates in regard to inner-city problems.
- ☐ Be an informed voter.
- ☐ Work for an alignment of federal and state resources to help the urban poor and to level the educational playing field.
- ☐ Be proactive in assuring that federal and state measures for success (i.e., testing) is free of bias or restrictions that single out any particular group.
- ☐ Work for national standards that take into account all students and that provide the resources for success—not just to the more affluent areas but also for all students and all teachers.
- ☐ Volunteer to serve on boards and committees, especially those that are setting policies for testing and for resources.

In the community

- ☐ Become proactive in the community to provide better health, mental, mentoring, physical, and fiscal resources for your students.
- ☐ Work with parents and other caregivers for solutions.
- ☐ Actively involve parents and members of the community in advisory groups.
- ☐ Set meetings at times that working parents can attend.
- ☐ Provide interpreters for parents who do not speak English.
- ☐ Take into consideration that some parents have come from countries where those in authority have not been fair or friendly. They may be wary of school personnel, especially if they are not citizens.
- ☐ Provide opportunities for your students to become proactive in their own communities with projects that include such activities as art, music, writing, starting a newsletter, providing help at clinics or other community facilities.
- ☐ Because poverty is a matter of lack of resources, help students increase the resources within their own communities.

In the hallways and within the school

- ☐ Make good nutrition a priority.
- ☐ Emphasize good hydration for learning.
- ☐ Examine curriculum and books for examples of bias and work toward a plan for eliminating bias throughout the school.
- ☐ Set norms that include the respect for all people.
- ☐ Set norms that say learning is important.
- ☐ Provide advisory groups that include students as well as community people.

- ☐ Provide opportunities for after-school activities.
- ☐ Provide opportunities for additional resources that are a part of the school budget, such as nurses, counselors, and librarians.
- ☐ Make sure that the resources in your school are rich in culture and that they reflect the races and ethnicities of your students. While Martin Luther King, Jr., Day is important, it should not be the only time of the year that we celebrate diversity.
- ☐ Be aware of students who are absent too much, are in danger of dropping out, in danger of failure, and so forth. Provide an adult advocate for every student in the school. (This can be done through teams of teachers and senior students.)
- ☐ Fight for better conditions for your school if they are not up to par with other schools in your region.
- ☐ Be proactive in asking for the resources that your students need to be successful.
- ☐ Provide ongoing professional development that includes ways to reach students in your school and that examines the best practices, especially in regard to brain research and learning.

In the classroom

- ☐ Set classroom standards that define expectations that all students will be respected.
- ☐ Bond with all of the students.
- ☐ Model the behavior that you expect of your students.
- ☐ Provide information to your students about resources available to them.
- ☐ Make your students aware of the need for good nutrition and hydration in regard to learning.
- ☐ Communicate caring and concern for all students.
- ☐ Communicate high expectations while keeping the threat level low.
- ☐ Help your students understand how their own brains work and how that affects all that they do.
- ☐ Build positive self-efficacy in your students.
- ☐ Teach the hidden rules to students and when they are used.
- ☐ Build positive self-esteem in your students.
- ☐ Provide a variety of teaching resources in the classroom that take into account the backgrounds, ethnicity, and race of your students.
- ☐ Use a variety of modalities in the classroom, especially visual and kinesthetic.
- ☐ Contextualize the lessons.
- ☐ Create experiences that help students make connections between prior learning and experiences and the new learning.
- ☐ Create opportunities for students to set personal goals for the learning.
- ☐ Explicitly show students how to use self-talk and other techniques to revise their goals when they encounter problems.
- ☐ Help students complete work at a quality level.
- ☐ Provide specific and prescriptive feedback on an ongoing basis to students.
- ☐ Teach in a variety of ways so that students learn in the way to which they are accustomed.
- ☐ Help students make the transition form the language of the street to the language of the classroom.
- ☐ Provide opportunities for students to work together in heterogeneous groups.
- ☐ Emphasize the gifts that all students bring to the table.
- ☐ Recognize and overcome linguistic bias.

- ☐ Recognize and overcome stereotyping bias.
- ☐ Recognize and overcome exclusion bias.
- ☐ Recognize and overcome fragmentation/isolation bias.
- ☐ Recognize and overcome selectivity bias.
- ☐ Recognize and overcome unreality bias.

In addition, provide opportunities for networks with other teachers in your building and in other schools to support and encourage you.

Stalin supposedly said that he did not need armies to take over countries. He said to give him the country's children for one generation and he would have the country. Who has greater influence over society than teachers? Our influence has the power to change a new generation—for the better.

References

Association for Supervision and Curriculum Development. (1999a). *ASCD yearbook.* Alexandria, VA: Author.

Barker, J. (1992). *Future edge.* New York: William Morrow.

Bloom, B. S. (1956). *Taxonomy of educational objectives, handbook I: Cognitive domain.* New York: McKay.

Bloom, B. S. (1976). *Human characteristics and school learning.* New York: McGraw-Hill.

Booth Sweeney, L. (2001). *When a butterfly sneezes: A guide for helping kids explore interconnections in our world through favorite stories.* Waltham, MA: Pegasus.

Bruer, J. T. (1993). *Schools for learning.* Cambridge: MIT Press.

Choiniere, R., & Keirsey, D. (1992). *Presidential temperament: The unfolding of character in the forty presidents of the United States.* Del Mar, CA: Prometheus Nemesis.

Covey, S. R. (1989). *Seven habits of highly effective people.* New York: Simon & Schuster.

Deming, W. E. (1986). *Out of the crisis.* Cambridge: MIT Press.

Diamond, M. (1998). *Enriching heredity: The impact of the environment on the anatomy of the brain.* New York: Free Press.

Diamond, M., Scheibel, A., Murphy, G., & Harvey, T. (1985). On the brain of a scientist: Albert Einstein. *Experimental Neurology, 88,* 198–204.

Ellis, A. K., & Fouts, J. T. (1997). *Research and educational innovations.* Larchmont, NY: Eye on Education.

Feuerstein, R. et al. (1980). *Instrumental enrichment: An intervention program for cognitive modifiability.* Glenview, IL: Scott, Foresman.

Fitzgerald, R. (1996). Brain compatible teaching in the block schedule. *The School Administrator, 8*(2), 20.

Foster, A. (1999). Telementoring: One way to reach America's students. *NASSP Bulletin* (Reston, VA: National Association of Secondary School Principals), *83*(608), 76–79.

Gibbs, J. (1994). *Tribes.* Santa Rosa, CA: Center Source.

Glasser, W. (1994, March–April). Teach students what they will need in life. *ATPE News,* pp. 20–21.

Goleman, D. (1995). *Emotional intelligence: Why it can matter more than IQ.* New York: Bantam Books.

Haberman, M. (1996). Characteristics of star teachers. *Instructional Leader, 9*(6), 1–3.

Hanson, J. M., & Childs, J. (1998). Creating a school where people like to be. *Educational Leadership, 50*(1), 14–16.

Henderson, N., & Milstein, M. (2003). *Resiliency in schools: Making it happen for students and educators.* Thousand Oaks, CA: Corwin Press.

Hooper, L. (1992, November 16). No compromises. *The Wall Street Journal,* p. R8.

Jacoby, P. (1991). *Region XIII Education Service Center.* Austin, TX: Region X Education Center.

Jensen, E. (1995). *The learning brain.* Del Mar, CA: Turning Point.

Jensen, E. (1997). *Completing the puzzle: The brain-compatible approach to learning.* Del Mar, CA: Turning Point.

Jensen, E. (1998). *Introduction to brain compatible learning.* Del Mar, CA: Turning Point.

Keefe, J. M. (1997). *Instruction and the learning environment.* Larchmont, NY: Eye on Education.

Kinneavy, J. L. (1991). Rhetoric. In J. Flood, J. M. Jensen, D. Lapp, & J. R. Squire (Eds.), *Handbook of research on teaching the English language arts.* New York: Macmillan.

Klenk, V. (1983). *Understanding symbolic logic.* Englewood Cliffs, NJ: Prentice-Hall.

Kotulak, R. (1996). *Inside the brain.* Kansas City, MO: Andrews McMeel.

Lawrence, T. E. (1935). *Seven pillars of wisdom.* New York: Random House.

Marlowe, B. A., & Page, M. L. (1998). *Creating and sustaining the constructivist classroom.* Thousand Oaks, CA: Corwin Press.

Marzano, R. J. (1992). *A different kind of classroom: Teaching with dimensions of learning.* Alexandria, VA: Association for Supervision and Curriculum Development.

Marzano, R. J. (1998). *A theory based meta-analysis of research on instruction.* Aurora, CO: Mid-Continent Regional Educational Laboratory.

Marzano, R. J. (2001a). *Designing a new taxonomy of educational objectives.* Thousand Oaks, CA: Corwin Press.

Marzano, R. J. (2001b). *What works in schools.* Alexandria, VA: Association for Supervision and Curriculum Development.

National Association of Secondary School Principals. (1996). *Breaking ranks: Changing an American institution.* Reston, VA: Author.

National Center for Research on Evaluation, Standards, and Student Testing. (n.d.). *National Center for Research on Evaluation, Standards, and Student Testing.* Retrieved October 31, 2004, from www.cresst.org.

Newmann, F. W., & Wehlage, G. G. (1993). Five standards of authentic instruction. *Educational Leadership, 50*(7), 8–12.

O'Neil, J. (1995). On lasting school reform: A conversation with Ted Sizer. *Educational Leadership, 52*(5), 12.

O'Tuel, F. S., & Bullard, P. K. (1993). *Developing higher order thinking in the content areas K–12.* Pacific Grove, CA: Critical Thinking Press.

Parks, S., & Black, H. (1992). *Organizing thinking* (Vol. 1). Pacific Grove, CA: Critical Thinking Press.

Payne, R. (1996). Understanding and working with students and adults from poverty. *The Instructional Leader, 9*(2), 3–5.

Payne, R. K. (2001) *A framework for understanding poverty.* Highlands, TX: Aha! Process.

Perry, B. D. (1995). *Children, youth, and violence: Searching for solutions.* New York: Guilford.

Pyle, G., & Andre, T. (1986). *Cognitive classroom learning—Understanding thinking and problem solving.* Orlando, FL: Academic Press.

Quindlen, A. (2004, September 20). The last word. *Newsweek,* p. 68.

Resnick, O. P., & Resnick, L. B. (1997). The nature of literacy: An historical exploration. *Harvard Educational Review, 47*(3).

Sousa, D. (1995). *How the brain learns.* Reston, VA: National Association of Secondary School Principals.

Sousa, D. (1997). *How the brain learns: New insights into the teaching/learning process* [Audiotape]. Reston, VA: National Association of Secondary School Principals.

Sousa, D. (2001). *How the brain learns* (2nd ed.). Thousand Oaks, CA: Corwin Press.

Sprenger, M. (1999). *Learning and memory: The brain in action.* Alexandria, VA: Association for Supervision and Curriculum Development.

Sprenger, M. (2002). *Becoming a "Wiz" at brain-based teaching.* Thousand Oaks, CA: Corwin Press.

Stiggins, R. J. (1994). *Student-centered classroom assessment* (2nd ed.). Columbus, OH: Merrill.

Tapscott, D. (1998). The net generation and the school. Retrieved February 11, 2005, from http://www.mff.org/edtech/article.taf.

Tileston, D. W. (2000). *Ten best teaching practices: How brain research, learning styles and standards define teaching standards.* Thousand Oaks, CA: Corwin Press.

Tileston, D. W. (2004a). *What every teacher should know about diverse learners.* Thousand Oaks, CA: Corwin Press.

Tileston, D. W. (2004b). *What every teacher should know about effective teaching strategies.* Thousand Oaks, CA: Corwin Press.

Tileston, D. W. (2004c). *What every teacher should know about learning, memory and the brain.* Thousand Oaks, CA: Corwin Press.

Tileston, D. W. (2004d). *What every teacher should know about media and technology.* Thousand Oaks, CA: Corwin Press.

Tileston, D. W. (2004e). *What every teacher should know about student assessment.* Thousand Oaks, CA: Corwin Press.

Toliver, K. (1995). *Good Morning Mrs. Toliver* [Videotape]. Los Angeles: KCET.

Torrence, E. P. (1966). *Torrence test of creative thinking.* Princeton, NJ: Personnel Press.

U.S. Department of Labor. (1991). *Scans: Blueprint for action.* Washington, DC: Author.

Walker, D. (1998). *Strategies for teaching differently: On the block or not.* Thousand Oaks, CA: Corwin Press.

Wang, M. C., & Kovach, J. A. (1996). Bridging the achievement gap in urban schools: Reducing educational segregation and advancing resilience-promoting strategies. In B. Williams (Ed.),*Closing the Achievement Gap* (pp. 10–36). Alexandria, VA: Association for Supervision and Curriculum and Development.

Werner, E. E., & Smith, R. S. (1992). *Overcoming the odds: High-risk children from birth to adulthood.* Ithaca, NY: Cornell University Press.

Whisler, N., & Williams, J. (1990). *Literature and cooperative learning: Pathway to literacy.* Sacramento, CA: Literature Co-op.

Wiggins, G., & McTighe, J. (1998). *Understanding by design.* Alexandria, VA: Association for Supervision and Curriculum Development.

Index

**CORWIN
PRESS**